A GLAMOROUS GUIDE TO LIVING BLONDE

Be Marilyn!

A GLAMOROUS GUIDE TO LIVING BLONDE

GAILYN ADDIS

SOURCEBOOKS, INC.®
NAPERVILLE, ILLINOIS

Dedicated to Mom.

Published by Sourcebooks, Inc.
1935 Brookdale Road, Suite 139, Naperville, Illinois 60563.
(630) 961-3900
Fax (630) 961-2168

Be Marilyn! A Glamorous Guide to Living Blonde is produced by
becker&mayer!, Ltd.
www.beckermayer.com

Design by Two Pollard Design.
Art direction by Simon Sung.
Edited by Stephanie Westcott and Sarah McCormic.
Production by Marypat Faraone.

Library of Congress Cataloging-in-Publication Data

Addis, Gailyn.
    Be Marilyn!: a glamorous guide to living blonde / Gailyn Addis.
        p.   cm.
    ISBN 1-57071-557-2 (acid-free paper)
    1. Monroe, Marilyn, 1926-1962—Miscellanea. I. Title.

PN2287.M69 A64 2000
791.43'028'092—dc21   00-026371

Printed in China
ISBN 1-57071-557-2

becker&mayer! 10 9 8 7 6 5 4 3 2 1

First Edition

Marilyn Monroe: A Brief Biography

Marilyn Monroe was born Norma Jeane Mortenson on June 1, 1926, in Los Angeles, California, to Gladys Monroe-Baker-Mortenson. Due to mental illness, which ran in the family (Della Monroe, Norma Jeane's grandmother, died of a manic seizure at the Norwalk Asylum in California in 1927), Gladys was unable to take care of Norma Jeane and put her under the care of Ida and Albert Wayne Bolender.

By March of 1933, Gladys had saved enough money to purchase a condo in the Hollywood Hills and felt well enough to take Norma Jeane with her. However, less than one year later, Gladys slipped back into the grips of the mental illness that plagued her and was committed to a mental hospital. Norma Jeane was almost eight years old. From then on, she would be in and out of foster homes, and even an orphanage, until her arranged marriage to first husband James Edward Dougherty at the age of sixteen in 1942.

In spite of what seemed to be a happy marriage, the absence of love, insecurity, and the lack of belonging that Norma Jeane experienced as a child had permanently scarred her. It was out of that emptiness and need that she developed a vivid imagination, a love for movies, and a dream of being a famous, beautiful movie star who would be loved and admired by everyone.

Her first break came in 1944. With husband Jim off to war, Norma Jeane joined the war effort herself and went to work for Radio Plane Company, packing parachutes. It was there that army photographer David Conover discovered her, and the photos he took changed her life forever. She went to Emmeline Snively's Blue Book Modeling Agency where she quickly became one of the most popular cover models in the country. She divorced Dougherty, and in July 1946, was signed to 20th Century Fox for a salary of $75.00 per week. She changed her name to Marilyn Monroe.

An early studio shot of the young Marilyn Monroe.

It was several years of struggles, disappointments, and small, forgettable film parts before "powerhouse" agent Johnny Hyde, who fell in love with Marilyn, gave her a firm footing in Hollywood with a better contract ($500.00/week) and better roles. Marilyn's subsequent rise to fame in the 1950s was accompanied by failed marriages to baseball great Joe DiMaggio and renowned playwright Arthur Miller, scandalous affairs and controversies, and an increased dependency on sleeping pills, barbiturates, and alcohol. In the midst of her personal anguish, she managed to find the motivation and desire to transform herself from the shallow, sexpot image that brought her to fame into a respected dramatic actress. She moved to New York and studied with renowned acting guru Lee Strasberg. She subsequently turned out several critically acclaimed films toward the end of her career. She died at age thirty-six on August 5, 1962, at her home in Los Angeles of what was said to be an overdose of sleeping pills.

Nearly forty years later, her image has become indelibly written in our minds as that which represents the epitome of glamour, sensuality, innocence, and femininity. This book is for all those who find themselves still mesmerized by the image, the woman behind the image, and the legend that is Marilyn Monroe.

Marilyn caught on film in a casual, off-screen moment.

Table of Contents

Be Marilyn!

INTRODUCTION

What do Cindy Crawford, Mira Sorvino, Theresa Russell, Madonna, Ashley Judd, Catherine Hicks, Lisa Marie Presley, and Bridget Fonda all have in common?

They all have in some way or another imitated or impersonated Marilyn Monroe.

Marilyn Monroe—our fascination with her never seems to wane. In fact, her popularity and our obsession with her continue to grow the further we move from the period in which she lived. But why do so many women (and sometimes men) want to be like her, look like her, imitate her smile and wave, her sexiness and softness? Beautiful models and actresses find themselves compelled to portray her in film and television or dress like her for Halloween, photo shoots, and publicity stunts. And why does the public gobble it up as if they've never seen a blonde bombshell before? Like Greta Garbo, Jean Harlow, and Rita Hayworth, Marilyn was certainly glamorous, and there is definitely something intangible about glamour that captures our imaginations. Marlene Dietrich, one of the great glamour queens of this century, said it best, "The word glamour means something indefinite, something inaccessible to normal women—an unreal paradise, desirable but basically out of reach." She was absolutely right.

Madonna copied the pink "Diamonds are a Girl's Best Friend" dress for her 1987 "Material Girl" video.

And even more so today. Never has fashion been so *unglamorous*. Raunch and grunge are in. Hats, gloves, brooches, and heels are something for school plays. False eyelashes, red lips, and painted brows are relegated to Halloween or underground clubs. But Marilyn, wonderful Marilyn, brought an approachability and warmth to the glamour that eludes so many of us. She was glamorous without appearing whorish or snobbish. She still somehow seems like the girl next door. And to this day, people still react to her image and her impersonators as if they were seeing their long lost sister, their best friend, or their lover.

So now the question is why *not* be like Marilyn, if only for the fun of it. Or for a new image. Or to do it professionally. Why should glamour be so elusive? For women of the new millennium, anything goes!

If I can do it, so can you.

3

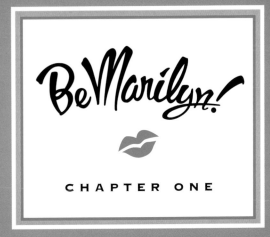

CHAPTER ONE

Matching Marilyn's

Magical Look

"...On the few occasions Marilyn did go out on the town, to premieres and the like, she became incredibly concerned about looking her best.

"The preparations would begin early in the morning with the arrival of Kenneth, the famous hairdresser....Sometimes Kenneth would be there for hours trying one approach after another. At each new vision she saw in her mirrors, Marilyn would scream, 'I hate it, I hate it.' Eventually, Kenneth somehow achieved the day's magic formula....The makeup sessions were equally agonizing. There were endless discussions over shades of lipstick and eye shadow, false eyelashes, rouge, and powder....Later in the day, after the hair and face were perfect, it was my turn to help Marilyn select clothes for the evening. Sadly, more than once Marilyn became so frustrated she began weeping, deciding not to go out at all....Yet when she did go out she looked wonderful. Marilyn was never happier than when she was able to go out in full regalia, and I was happy whenever she had the chance no matter how much work was involved."

Lena Pepitone, Marilyn's
wardrobe mistress in New York

Marilyn applying face cream.

Looking at the photos of the beautifully radiant Marilyn, with her sort of tousled yet perfectly polished style (which was her own invention), it's hard to believe that her goddess look that still transfixes us today was actually quite drawn out and involved. I guess we just expect her to have rolled out of bed ready for a photo shoot or for "lights, camera, action!" In fact, photos of Marilyn without makeup show her to be still naturally lovely, but what was it about her face that made her so special? Bert Stern also searched for the answer in his book *The Last Sitting*: "My eye roved her face, searching. I couldn't find the secret of her beauty in any one feature. She didn't have a great nose like Liz Taylor, or perfect lips like Brigitte Bardot. She didn't have gorgeous almond-shaped eyes like Sophia Loren. And yet she was more to me than all of them put together."

This black halter dress from Macy's became my first Marilyn costume.

The answer to the question may lie in some of Marilyn's less obvious but still wonderful features, not least of which was her flawless skin. As a young teen, Norma Jeane washed her face as much as fifteen times a day to keep it clean and prevent blemishes. Her complexion had an even, creamy white tone that looked luminescent and sometimes even ethereal on camera. She had facial hair in the form of a thin layer of white fuzz that apparently would catch the light and make her appear to glow. Otis Guernsey, a reporter for the *New York Herald Tribune*, said of *Gentlemen Prefer Blondes*, "Marilyn looks as though she would glow in the dark."

She avoided the sun, saying she liked to feel "blonde all over." But while she was living in New York, there was a time when she allowed herself to get a tan. Longtime fan and author James Haspiel has rare photos confirming this in his book *Marilyn*. In addition, later photos from the filming of *The Misfits* by photojournalist Eve Arnold and ones taken one month before her death by George Barris (photographer and author of *Marilyn: Her Life in Her Own Words*) show a freckled Marilyn. But in footage and wardrobe test photos from her last unfinished movie, *Something's Got to Give*, she appeared with her classic, radiant, white-on-white complexion.

Marilyn made only $18,000 for her role in *Gentlemen Prefer Blondes*. Her costar, Jane Russell, made $100,000.

My "Diamonds" dress is made out of soft satin, but Marilyn's was made out of a much stiffer pink upholstery.

As for Marilyn's facial features, her rounded face, the wide distance between her eyes, her high, wide forehead, and her full lips and button nose were actually more proportionate to those of a child. Baby pictures of most people will reveal those same qualities, but most of us mature quite differently than Marilyn. Her baby face combined with her sensuality and vulnerability to make her irresistible. At the top center of her forehead she had a pronounced widow's peak, which made her forehead appear heart-shaped. Her cheeks were full and plump. There was a longer-than-average distance between her eyebrows and the bottom of her eyelid, which gave her that eyes-half-closed look—one of her trademarks. Her nose, with the

help of a little surgery early on—compliments of super agent Johnny Hyde (she also had some cartilage placed in her chin)—had a button look with a little round bulb at the end, another trademark. Ironically, her lips were very flat, but she would spend hours redrawing and shading them to look full and moist to the point where some thought her mouth was her best feature. Of course, her teeth were near perfect, but she had worn a retainer and had some minor cosmetic dentistry done in her early years as a starlet. She was also obsessive about going to the dentist to keep them clean and free from cavities.

A fresh-faced Marilyn before her hair was straightened.

When Marilyn was placed under the hot spotlights and in front of the camera—her round baby face with the skin aglow, the eyes half closed, her moist, luscious mouth slightly open, her rosy cheeks, her contradictory zest for life yet ever-lingering sadness, her unforced sensuality—it's not at all hard to understand her appeal.

Now, given all that I've just said, you're either thinking, "I don't stand a chance!" or perhaps you see in yourself some Marilynesque potential. You don't have to be a dead ringer to do this, and if you're lacking in certain features, I'll show you how you can create the illusion that you are not (Marilyn was an expert at this). Even if you only want to be more glamorous and not necessarily a Marilyn impersonator, these makeup steps will work for you.

"The thought of being a Marilyn impersonator never entered my mind, but I was pushed into a Marilyn Monroe look-alike contest. It was the first time that I ever fixed myself up to look like her. I must admit it felt a little strange at first and I wondered if people would be upset at me for doing this. My biggest fear was that they'd start throwing tomatoes at me. But instead everyone was excited to meet me and cheered me on."

Diana Dawn,
Marilyn Monroe impersonator,
San Francisco

Preparation

"You don't just wake up in the morning and wash your face and comb your hair and go out in the street and look like Marilyn Monroe. She knows every trick of the beauty trade."

Milton Greene,
photographer

Marilyn was very good at applying her own makeup. She studied her face for hours and knew how to shade and highlight with the best of them. Still, she called upon her personal makeup artists when she had important events to attend and wanted to look her best. And, in fact, that is the best way to make sure your makeup is flawless. However, a good makeup artist can be expensive, and I'd be broke if I hired one every time I had a gig. So I've learned how to do it myself. The best way for me to teach you is to explain what I do.

Here I have imitated an exact pose from a Marilyn studio shot taken at 20th Century Fox.

1. As I pull back my hair and look at my face's shape, it is clear that my face is not as wide and round as Marilyn's. So I use highlighting to change that. Although I do have a small widow's peak, it is not as pronounced. Marilyn had her hairline permanently heightened by electrolysis. But I don't care to go to that extreme. Waxing also is not a good idea, because the hair may not grow back (so don't wax your hairline unless you're certain you don't want that hair anymore). Instead, I simply use hair gel to push my hair as far off my face as possible, and make sure that no dark roots are visible.

2. Next are the eyebrows. I have them waxed as thin as I can stand it because I will be drawing them above their natural line to make the distance from brow to lid appear as long as Marilyn's.

3. Now the skin. I take care of my skin by staying out of the sun and washing it frequently. (Gee, I wonder where I got that idea?) I also occasionally have dermatological facials to remove blemishes. My skin is oily, so I have to use an oil-free makeup, although Marilyn's skin never appeared dry, but quite moist. In fact, she frequently wore oils and heavy creams such as olive oil, lanolin, Vaseline, or hormone cream all over her face to prevent dryness. She actually did this in public as well. During the filming of *River of No Return* in Canada, makeup artist Whitey Snyder told Marilyn to stop wearing her hormone cream in public because she was "scaring people."

The right lighting helps to create the illusion.

Marilyn first wore makeup when she was ten years old. Apparently, the head-mistress of the orphanage where Norma Jeane lived put a little powder and lipstick on her to cheer her up. The young Norma Jeane was thrilled. By the time she was fifteen, she was doing her makeup by herself.

Applying the Makeup

When making up as Marilyn, I start with the eyes instead of the base. I don't want powder from my eye shadow or flakes of mascara marking my perfectly laid foundation.

1. I apply an under-eye moisture cream.

2. I apply white cream concealer/highlighter all over my eyelids and blend in well.

3. With a medium shadow brush, I dust an off-white eye shadow over the entire eyelid.

4. With a smaller shadow brush, I take a natural-toned shadow and highlight slightly above my eye crease just under my brow bone to create the illusion that my natural eye crease is higher than it really is. If I were working on a big stage with bright spotlights, I would darken that newly formed crease with a natural brown shadow—that goes for the eyebrows as well—but up close and personal, I like to keep it less dramatic.

5. Then I apply mascara and brush the lashes in the inner corner downward and brush the lashes in the outer corner upward. I don't find it necessary to apply eyeliner (which can be a mess to work with anyway), since the next step, applying the eyelashes, automatically creates the illusion of eyeliner.

6. For false eyelashes, I use black demi-wispies, Ardel Invisibands™—available at most beauty supply stores and drugstores—and mold them slightly with my hands before applying to fit the shape of my eye and create Marilyn eyes. I bend the inner corner downward and the

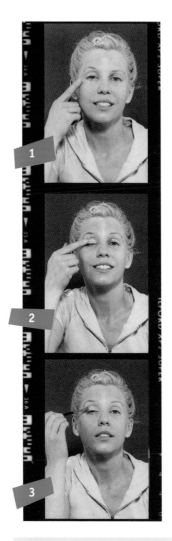

"Marilyn has makeup tricks no-body else has and nobody else knows....She has certain ways of lining and shadowing her eyes that no other actress can do."

Allan "Whitey" Snyder, makeup artist

outer corner upward. Using Duo Dark™ eyelash glue, I apply the lash starting from the inner edge of my iris outward, pressing the lash downward in the inner and center part of the eye while making sure the outer corner is flipped upward. This takes practice, so don't be frustrated if you don't get it right the first time. Be sure to have cotton swabs on hand to clean up mistakes. (*Now she tells us!*)

7. Now I'm ready to apply my foundation. I use an oil-free base in an ivory shade (see a cosmetician to find the shade and type that's right for you) and apply it quite heavily—even to my neck and chest—to hide freckles.

8. Then I apply an under-eye concealer (again, you'll have to find your proper shade).

9. With a light brown eyebrow pencil, I draw the Marilyn eyebrows, starting from the inside corner of my eye (again, this helps create the appearance that my eyes are wider set), above my own, bringing them to a point at the arch. I fill them in with a pencil, then brush the brows upward with a clear mascara.

10. Before contouring, you may want to dust your face lightly with powder so the contouring goes on smoothly. Because my foundation has a powdery finish, I don't need to do this. Also, the areas I need to contour will vary from yours. You can use what I do as a frame of reference, but if you're still not sure, use a good black-and-white photo of Marilyn as your guideline. My contouring involves simply using a small shadow brush and drawing a light tan contour powder on the inside corner of my eyes. This makes the bridge of my nose seem flatter. Then I literally draw on the round bulb on the end of my nose and put a little shading inside my nostrils to make them appear a little more flared.

"...Her eyelashes were a pain in the neck to me. She liked to wear loads of them. I had to hand trim them for her because there were no ready-trimmed eyelashes then. Marilyn knew how I hated this chore, so when she was mad at me she always gave me several extra pairs of eyelashes to trim as my punishment."

George Masters,
hairdresser and
makeup artist

11. For the blush, I prefer peach and orange tones. I brush it on under my cheekbone horizontally to keep my face looking wide. Smiling like Marilyn helps me to find where to put it. I also dust it lightly around my temples and forehead.

12. Using a true red lip liner (make sure it is an orange red and not a pink red), I draw my lip line well above my own and fill it in with an orange-red lipstick. I add highlights to both upper and lower lips with a beige lip gloss, creating a full, luscious look.

13. One last touch before the mole. I dust a light, shimmery powder all over my face, emphasizing my cheeks, chin, and forehead. With my finger, I put some extra on my eyelids and just under my eyebrow. Marilyn told Susan Strasberg, daughter of Lee Strasberg and author of the book *Marilyn and Me*, to put Vaseline™ on her cheeks and lips to make them shine for her role in *Picnic*. In fact, Marilyn was known to have put saliva on her cheeks to make them shine when Vaseline™ wasn't available. I've tried the Vaseline,

and it works for the camera, but up close and personal, people would probably think you'd rubbed your face in a plate of greasy french fries. (As for the saliva—that's something you'll have to try yourself!)

14. Finally, I draw the mole on the left side of my face, just outside of my smile line, using a black waterproof, smudgeproof pencil. There seems to be a little controversy surrounding Marilyn's mole. Some photos show it on the right side of her face, and in some early Norma Jeane photos it is not evident at all. The truth is she did have a small mole on the left side of her face about which she said, "Sometimes I darken it, sometimes I don't." Photos that show it on the right side were printed from the reverse side of the negatives. In *Some Like It Hot* and *Let's Make Love*, it was covered up with makeup and drawn on the left side of her chin.

"I thought she must use fluorescent makeup, the way she'd shine."

Delos Smith Jr., actor

Gentlemen Really Do Prefer Blondes!

"There are several problems with doing Marilyn's hair. Her hair is very fine and hard to manage. It gets oily if it isn't shampooed every day. And her hair is so curly naturally that to build a coiffure for her I have to first give her a straight permanent....The way we got her shade of platinum is with my own secret blend of sparkling silver bleach plus twenty volume peroxide and a secret formula of silver platinum to take the yellow out."

Gladys Rasmussen, hairdresser

Wearing a wig and blending my own hair in works best for me.

16

By now, it is common knowledge how the young Norma Jeane, a wavy-haired brunette, had her hair lightened and straightened by hairdresser Sylvia Barnhart at the recommendation of Emmeline Snively, Marilyn's first

modeling agent in Hollywood. But she went through many styles and shades of blonde before arriving at the classic coiffure we remember most today. When she was an ingenue, her hair fell well below her shoulders. Early films such as *Scudda Hoo! Scudda Hay!*, *Ladies of the Chorus, Love Happy,* and *A Ticket to Tomahawk* revealed a starlet with long, wavy hair. In *All About Eve,* Marilyn's hair was pulled back, giving her a more mature look. Although her hair was shorter and curlier in *Don't Bother to Knock, As Young As You Feel, We're Not Married,* and *Monkey Business,* it was a darker shade of blonde.

Finally, three films, all released in 1953, unveiled the Marilyn do that would become her trademark and launch her into full-fledged stardom. *Niagara, Gentlemen Prefer Blondes,* and *How to Marry a Millionaire* showcased Marilyn in a short, platinum, slightly layered bob, with hair curled under in the back and on the sides (most of the time), parted on the extreme left side of her head, arched high above her forehead, with a few curls falling loosely around the temples.

Marilyn was petrified of the camera. Her fear caused her to be late or sometimes not to show up at all— and even throw up before her scenes.

As far as who is responsible for creating Marilyn's coif, Sydney Guilaroff takes credit for the blunt cut she sported in *The Asphalt Jungle*, and George Masters claims to have given her locks the perfect shade of platinum—what Marilyn called "pillow case white." As for that single, loose curl that typically fell softly above her right temple, that reportedly was the result of hairdressers' efforts to hide the dark roots to the right of her pronounced cowlick, which did not take well to the peroxide. Other hairstylists responsible for shaping her famous tresses included Kenneth Battelle, whom she called upon frequently from 1958 until her death in 1962, Agnes Flanagan, Peter Leonardi, and Gladys Rasmussen.

Not many things in Marilyn's life were simple, and as you've probably guessed, her hairstyling process was no exception. Her hair required bleaching once a week, and early photos show her hair being styled using pin curls. Her hair was curled, then rigorously teased to give it a tousled or natural look, then sprayed and set to last for a couple of days. Before she became a star, she is known to have phoned friends as early as 3:00 A.M. (her early-morning phone calls to friends would become more and more frequent) to ask whether or not she should wash her hair for an interview the next day. Much later, after she fled to New York with the aid of photographer Milton Greene, she became increasingly particular about her hair.

"Try lemon for your hair, or beer. It's even better, you know, for the highlights on camera. If it doesn't work, you can drink it…as soon as you're legal, of course."

Marilyn Monroe to
Susan Strasberg

This is a knock-off gown I picked up at a resale shop.

For special occasions, Marilyn would sometimes make her hairdressers style and restyle her hair until she was happy. (This was due to insecurity and her desire to live up to her image rather than any desire to be difficult.) However, when she wasn't doing movies or special appearances, she tended to go for days at a time without bathing or washing her hair. (No intention to dish the dirt here—it's just that our beautiful, squeaky clean Marilyn was human. In fact, that's what makes us adore her so much.)

In *The Seven Year Itch* and *Bus Stop*, Marilyn's hair was a little shorter and curlier, while her "Happy Birthday, Mr. President" and *Something's Got to Give* look during the months before her death was a whiter, straighter, heavily teased bob with a dramatic flip.

Marilyn's hairdo in 1962.

Gentlemen Prefer You!

"As a general rule Marilyn would begin turning on about eight hours after I had started with her, while I was applying her lipstick or adjusting her dress. Until then she was a girl you wouldn't look twice at. When she became secure enough to turn into this other person named Marilyn Monroe, then all of a sudden something happened. That's when it was goose-bump time."

George Masters, hairstylist

In styling your own hair to emulate Marilyn, you have several choices: wear a wig, bleach your own hair, or both. If you want to be a professional look-alike but don't want to bleach your hair, you can have a special lace-front wig made—but the cost could be anywhere from $300 to $500. If your forehead is high enough, you may be able to get by with a regular wig. If you bleach your own hair but want to prevent damage from frequent styling and teasing, you may want to wear a `wig *and* have bleached hair but only pull out the front of your own hair to blend with the rest of the wig.

Marilyn in a publicity shot for The Seven Year Itch, *1955.*

To tell you the truth, I've tried all of the above. I had auburn hair when I started, and just wore a regular wig. Not having the critical eye I now have, I didn't realize that I looked like I was wearing a yellow helmet. Later, I was fortunate enough to work for Universal Studios, and they made me a lace-front wig. This is a special wig where a mold is made of your head, and your natural hairline is drawn. Then the wigmaker sews a fine, flesh-toned net onto the front of a Marilyn-type wig and then meticulously sews individual strands of hair around the hairline. The effect created is that the hair appears to be growing out of your head. Now, finally, I have platinum hair myself. Even though the lace-front wig looked great, I found that when I was meeting the different agents or producers who had hired me for a job, especially the ones overseas, they would see me out of costume with my auburn hair and pretty soon I would see them all studying me with furrowed brows and whispering among themselves. I guess they were concerned that they were not getting what they had paid for. (Some people have no imagination.) So, in order not to worry my clients, I decided to go blonde and keep up the image even when I wasn't actually performing. But, for my actual shows or appearances, I still wear a wig, and pull my own hair out of the front and blend it in.

Now, I want to caution those of you who want to impersonate Marilyn professionally. I personally feel that the hair is the most important part of the look. I'm certain it is the most scrutinized. Audiences will be studying it carefully, wondering, "Is that her *real* hair?" People frequently ask me, "Is that *your* hair?" I answer, wide-eyed, empty-headed, and in my full Marilyn voice, "Of course it is… and I have the receipt to prove it!"

Advertising Her Secrets

Marilyn did print ads for some hair products, including a Hiltone Hair ColorTM ad that read "Marilyn Monroe says, 'Gentlemen prefer blondes, and blondes prefer New Hiltone with the cream foam action.'" She also did ads for Westmore Hollywood Cosmetics™ and Lustre Cream Shampoo.™ Even then, women wanted to know Marilyn's beauty secrets and the products she used.

CHAPTER TWO

Captivating Costumes

Part One: Underneath It All

"I'd rather be either really dressed up or really undressed. I don't bother with anything in between."

Marilyn Monroe

Racy talk like this got Marilyn a lot of publicity back in the more modest era of the 1950s, but given reports from friends, employees, and even just acquaintances, Marilyn really did like to lounge around in her birthday suit. It seemed to relax her, even put her in a hypnotic state, according to acting teacher Natasha Lytess, with whom Marilyn once boarded. Marilyn was quite comfortable with her notoriously voluptuous body, with proportions that by today's standards of beauty would be too large. Having a healthy appetite and being no immediate threat to Kate Moss, I take comfort in the fact that Marilyn Monroe was and is considered beautiful for her full figure. It has been said that Marilyn is the last star of our time allowed to have a tummy—allowed to have the figure of a woman. For those of us who aren't planning on sprouting into six-foot-tall, Twiggy-like runway models any time soon, it is good to know that Marilyn is in the public eye as much as ever, showing the world that it's OK for a girl to have hips.

This looks like a 1950s–era swimsuit, but I found it at a department store in the 1990s.

Much has been said and written about Marilyn's tantalizing torso and how she developed it, maintained it, enhanced it. By most accounts, she was 5 feet 5 ½ inches tall and weighed 117 pounds at the beginning of her career. At her death, she weighed approximately the same. In between, however, there was fluctuation upward as much as 20 pounds (again, I find comfort). Her weight even fluctuated during the making of the same film. *The Prince and the Showgirl* costume designer Beatrice Dawson said that two of each costume had to be made because Marilyn would indulge in eating so much on the days between shootings that she would come back one size larger. They would then put her on diuretics to try to get her weight back down. (This is neither practiced nor recommended by the author.)

"*Her whole body had a touch of overripeness— how Renoir would have adored her! She was indeed a little overweight and was worried very much about her tummy protruding in her tight white dress.*"

Jack Cardiff,
cinematographer

Of course, her exact measurements also fluctuated. According to the Blue Book Modeling Agency in 1945, they were 36"-24"-34." In the early 1950s, 20th Century Fox said they were 36 1/2"-23"-34," and 38"-23"-36" in 1955. Billy Travilla, Marilyn's most frequently used costume designer, has her measurements as 35"-22"-35." By studying her photos and watching her movies carefully, I have come to the brilliant conclusion that at her thinnest, Marilyn was probably 35"-22"-35" (I'm using Billy Travilla's measurement because he was her costume designer and undoubtedly wielded his tape measure frequently). For films where she appeared heavier, except *Some Like It Hot*, she fluctuated upward toward the 36- and 38-inch measurements. In *Some Like It Hot*, however, her bust and hips appear to be as much as 40 inches. According to Lena Pepitone, her wardrobe mistress at that time, Marilyn didn't want to be in *Some Like It Hot*, so she ate out of depression and hoped they wouldn't use her because she was too heavy. (She was also pregnant, but in early enough stages that it likely would not have shown.) Lucky for us, her scheme didn't work, and the movie became one of her best pieces of work and her most successful film. (Listen and learn, Kate Moss wanna-bes!)

My version of the "Happy Birthday, Mr. President" look.

Aside from her weight and measurements, Marilyn's actual breast size, density, and shape have been the topic of much discussion. And like most normal women, her breast size fluctuated along with the rest of her. For the most part, however, Marilyn was no more than a B-C cup. Early nude photos—including the famous "Golden Dreams" calendar shots, as well as her last sitting with Bert Stern—show that she had quite normal breasts. When people tell me she was a full D cup, that's when I know that either the myth about Marilyn is taking over the reality or the only movies they ever saw were *Some Like It Hot* and *The Misfits,* where she was overweight. Regardless of all that has been said—and most importantly—Marilyn knew how to use whatever she had, whenever she had it, to her utmost benefit. The exquisite and sensuous way she carried herself and the way she wore her clothes to enhance every nuance and curve made her appear more voluptuous than she already was.

This Lycra™ skirt is great for a fluctuating figure.

27

Another reality is that Marilyn had to work to keep her figure or at least to keep her weight down. She loved to eat and when she was depressed she would eat even more. She ate (and drank) whatever she wanted, and although she lifted weights and even went jogging early  on as a starlet, there's no evidence of much activity later on—especially after her flight to New York in Christmas 1954. From this time forward, she became less active, although she diligently fought to become a serious actress, studied with Lee Strasberg, and completed five more films. (She had made twenty-four films during her first eight years in Hollywood.) In the early days, when she had little money for food, she said she ate raw hamburger, grapefruit, and peanut butter and jelly—surviving on under a dollar a day. Natasha Lytess, Marilyn's first acting coach, reported that "Marilyn ate the same thing every morning when she was living with me: orange juice and gelatin, cold oatmeal, porridge with milk, and two eggs." Years later, while staying with her in New York, Lena Pepitone said that every day Marilyn ate three poached eggs, toast, and a Bloody Mary. She also loved steaks, lamb chops, Italian sausages, and spaghetti. In the Milton Greene household (Marilyn lived with photographer Greene and his family during her first year in New York), cook Kitty Owens said that "she [Marilyn] liked vegetables, including stewed tomatoes and corn, string beans, red cabbage with apples, and squash of every kind. She loved chili and her favorite was scrambled eggs with rolled anchovies and capers. But if Amy Greene caught her eating such fatty foods, she would snatch the plate away and say, 'You're on a diet, Marilyn. You're too fat now!'"

M.M. Productions

Perhaps the most notorious of all of Marilyn's photographers, Milton Greene helped orchestrate Marilyn's move from Los Angeles to New York in 1954. There, Marilyn lived with Milton and his wife, Amy, for about one year. Greene supported Marilyn financially, managed her business affairs, and became partners with her in Marilyn Monroe Productions. He negotiated a new contract for her with 20th Century Fox wherein she was to receive $100,000 per film, script and director approval, and the freedom to work for other studios. (This was considered an outstanding contract for any actor at that time.) Greene is credited by many for the success of Bus Stop and The Prince and the Showgirl, but after the latter, the partnership dissolved. Marilyn bought out Greene's share of M.M. Productions for $100,000.

Marilyn did feel bad about her weight gain during *Some Like It Hot* and put herself on a diet of fruits and vegetables to look good for its premiere. (One interesting body-sculpting exercise that she reportedly did was to stand in a bucket of ice until it melted. She said this made her legs firm. She also took ice baths with Chanel No. 5.) Still, on the night of the premiere, she almost didn't go, calling herself a fat pig. But after assurance from then-husband Arthur Miller and the rest of her entourage, she changed her mind. Photos of that night show her weight was down considerably, and she looked beautiful as usual. After making *The Misfits*, the last movie she would complete, Marilyn divorced Miller, moved back to Hollywood, and had her gallbladder removed. By the time she began filming on *Something's Got to Give*, her body was lean and beautiful and she looked more radiant than ever.

Marilyn appears slimmer than ever in this costume test for Something's Got to Give *in 1962.*

"I love food as long as it has flavor. It's flavorless food I can't stand. I usually have a steak and a green salad for my dinner, also for breakfast when I'm really hungry. I keep away from pastries—I used to love them, and ice cream, too. I skip all desserts unless it's fruit. I just don't like the taste of pastries. As a kid I did, but now I hate it— and as for candy, I can take it or leave it, usually leave it. But I love champagne—just give me champagne and good food, and I'm in heaven and love. That's what makes the world go round."

Marilyn Monroe

In the early 1960s, Marilyn was at her all-time thinnest, as photos reveal (see *Marilyn, Her Life in Her Own Words* by George Barris). With Marilyn eating as much meat as she reportedly did, it's hard to believe that even at age thirty-six her body looked great and she had no cellulite. One weakness she didn't have was a craving for sweets. She stayed away from candy even as a teenager and favored more hearty meals. But before you switch your diet to raw hamburger (she's lucky she didn't get sick), steaks, eggs, champagne, and Italian sausage, consult your doctor.

Happily Every After...

It's 10:30 P.M. on a hot, muggy Saturday night in the heart of Hollywood. I've just driven two hours from a gig. I'm exhausted, my bladder is full, and my fuel tank is empty. A huge concert has just let out at the Hollywood Bowl and traffic is at a standstill, backed up in all directions for miles. X@*X!!! How could I have gotten myself into this mess? My frustration builds. I can't take this traffic, this big city, the exhaust fumes. Suddenly, I hear a horn honking and girls screaming and shouting. I look around. A car full of girls, out for fun on a Saturday night, has spotted me. "Look—it's Marilyn!" "It's Marilyn Monroe!" "Hi, Marilyn!" "We love you, Marilyn!" I can't help but let my face break into a Marilynesque smile, and I wave back. They shriek with joy and amusement and drive away. Traffic dissipates, along with my tantrum, and another night as Marilyn has a happy ending.

Puttin' on the Glitz

As far as what Marilyn actually wore, as stated before, she liked to lounge around in either nothing or a white terry-cloth robe. But her costumes, evening wear, clothing for photo shoots, and even what she just wore out on appointments, could be extremely complicated and take hours and even days to put together. (Maybe that explains why the rest of the time she kept it so simple.) Even as a little girl, Norma Jeane was well-clad. Her foster mothers managed to sew her clothes or Gladys' (her real mother) allowance provided for her. By the time Norma Jeane was in high school, she was wearing formfitting sweaters and skirts. During her marriage to Jim Dougherty, she dressed well enough to catch the attention of many of the servicemen on Catalina Island where the couple resided when Dougherty was first called to duty. He recalls that Marilyn frequently wore all-white dresses or a white skirt and blouse with a colored ribbon in her hair and had the "cleanest kind of beauty" he'd ever seen, although he sometimes felt she wore things too tight and too sexy. (You don't say!)

When Norma Jeane was discovered by Army photographer David Conover, she was photographed in overalls and a tight red sweater. She wore a white sharkskin dress for her first interview with Emmeline Snively. Later on, after becoming a model with the Blue Book Modeling Agency, she had to buy many of her own clothes to pose in, as models did in those days. She had pairs of short tap-pant-style shorts; knee-length knickers; tight, cropped, short-sleeved and long-sleeved sweaters; two-piece strapless and halter swimsuits; one-piece

swimsuits; halter dresses; and pairs of strappy high heels and wedges. In several different photo sessions, she can be seen wearing a white pair of shorts with suspenders and a red-striped shirt, and a two-piece yellow halter bathing suit. In those early days, Norma Jeane was

Norma Jeane before she became a blonde known as Marilyn Monroe.

photographed mainly in swimsuits and tight shorts and sweaters and very little jewelry. It is also evident from photos taken at this time that she did very little padding. In some swimsuit shots she looked downright flat (she had also not entirely mastered the posing posture that would show her figure off so well in the years to come), but in the tight-sweater shots, it appears that Marilyn is wearing pointed brassieres—the style of the day. Later on, she more than likely padded her breasts a good deal of the time. Cinematographer Jack Cardiff recalled a conversation he had with Marilyn during the filming of *The Seven Year Itch*, in a scene where Marilyn was wearing a nightdress and appeared to be wearing a bra. "People don't wear bras under nightclothes," he told her. "Marilyn replied, 'What bra?' and put my hand on her breast. She was not wearing a bra.

"Her bosom was a miracle of shape, density, and an apparent lack of gravity." However, during the making of her last, unfinished movie, *Something's Got to Give*, Marilyn complained to producer Henry Weinstein that costar Cyd Charisse was padding her breasts. The producer said, "We're shooting her in a negligee. How [could she] pad the breasts?" And Marilyn said, "You're naive. You pad from underneath with tape!" Now, if you watch closely in the scene from *The Seven Year Itch* where Marilyn falls off the piano bench with Tom Ewell, when she gets up, you can see clearly down her dress and see the tape. I'm not saying she padded all the time. But given this statement and the visible evidence, it is probable she did so at least some of the time.

Thank heaven for the Miracle Bra™!

After her first contract with 20th Century Fox and her official name change to Marilyn Monroe, she began to dress a little more glamorously, having access to the studio's wardrobe department. As a young starlet in Hollywood, it is reported by more than one source, Marilyn wore halters, or loose-fitting blouses with a décolletage, skirts, and halter dresses—all one or two sizes too small. Wearing tight-fitting clothes was a trend that began with the young Norma Jeane and continued throughout her career. She also wore castoffs, or dresses previously worn by other stars, including Betty Grable. But Marilyn soon developed her own style of dressing, essentially the same as everyone else was wearing, only tighter and lower cut. A magazine in the early 1950s proclaimed that Marilyn was one of the worst-dressed women in Hollywood. But Marilyn defended herself by saying, "I dress for men, not for women; the latter look at clothes to criticize them, the former admire them. I wear as little as possible within the limits permitted by decency and…the law."

Decent and lawful!

The Costumes

There was really nothing too revealing about the costumes Marilyn wore in her earliest films, however. It wasn't until *Niagara* was released in 1953 that complaints arose that a red dress she donned in the movie was indecent. It was an off-the-shoulder, formfitting, below-the-knee dress that revealed a little of Marilyn's upper torso. By today's standards, it seems pretty modest, although things that wouldn't look sexy on most girls looked sexy on Marilyn.

The infamous pleated gold lamé gown.

Next came *Gentlemen Prefer Blondes* (1953), where Marilyn is decked out in three of her most famous costumes. Costume designer Billy Travilla had been instructed by the studio to create costumes that would prevent Marilyn's and Jane Russell's breasts from bouncing. So the costumes from their dance numbers had wire sewn into the busts to keep them stiff. Furthermore, no cleavage was to be shown. Miraculously, the costumes were still gorgeous, creative, and sexy. In fact, the most famous dress from the movie—the pink strapless "Diamonds Are a Girl's Best Friend" gown with the huge bow on the back, matching gloves, and tons of faux diamond jewelry—was not the costume Travilla originally designed for the number. He had first created an outfit in which Marilyn was adorned in only a fishnet stocking from head to toe with diamond jewelry barely covering her private parts. Knowing it would never make it past the censors, the studio instructed Travilla to design something that covered Marilyn completely and could not be

construed in the least as being sexy. Thus, he found the heaviest, stiffest pink drapery fabric he could find and created the now legendary pink gown, and Marilyn's sex appeal still came through with flying colors.

Next, there is the long-sleeve, red-sequined gown with the slit high up the leg, worn in the opening scene with Jane Russell. Both these dresses can be seen in miniature on Marilyn Monroe collector dolls.

Last but not least is the gold lamé pleated halter gown with the deep-plunging neckline that Marilyn actually had to be sewn into. Now, this dress was only in one scene in the movie, where Marilyn is dancing with Piggy, and, furthermore, it was only filmed from the back—it was considered too sexy for the film. But that didn't stop Marilyn from wearing it to a ceremony held in her honor at the Beverly Hills Hotel in 1953 when she was voted the Best New Actress of the Year by *Photoplay* magazine. She sang "Diamonds Are a Girl's Best Friend," and the dress reportedly split at the seams and had to be sewn up again. Her then-friend Joan Crawford ridiculed Marilyn to the press, accusing her of "throwing sex in people's faces."

The first costume designed by Billy Travilla for Diamonds are a Girl's Best Friend *was too revealing for the censors. I'm wearing a copy of the one that they finally approved.*

All of these dresses make excellent costumes for impersonators. (I recommend that you not be poured into them, though!) But you probably won't find them on the rack, so hopefully you have a good seamstress. *Gentlemen Prefer Blondes* also finds Marilyn in some of her most colorful suits and day wear, much of which is in style today, and is worth watching to get ideas for your own wardrobe.

How to Marry a Millionaire (1953), also showcases some famous Marilyn garb—in particular, a long, burgundy red satin gown with a single strap crossing one shoulder and a train draping down the back. The oft replayed scene shows Marilyn posing in front of a four-way mirror. (Five Marilyns in one shot!) Again, in spite of the fact that her character is supposed to be broke, Marilyn's wardrobe in the movie is full of gorgeous designer fur-trimmed suits, dresses, and glamorous hats and gloves.

The movie *River of No Return* (1954) was a departure for Marilyn from the "dumb blonde" roles. She still played a showgirl, but with a lot more savvy and street smarts—since it was a western, maybe "trail smarts." Her stage costumes were of the time period but still very Marilyn—long and sequined, figure-forming, off-the-shoulder gowns with slits high up the leg, accompanied by a large feathered headpiece. But, interestingly enough, what has become the most famous costume from this movie, due to an advertising campaign by Levi's™, is the pair of jeans and the simple, flowered, button-down blouse she wore for most of the movie.

Back to the glamour, *There's No Business Like Show Business* (1954) again finds Marilyn dressed to the hilt in every scene. My personal favorite is the long, white-sequined gown she wore while singing "After You Get What You Want You Don't Want It"—another great costume to emulate.

Marilyn was completely disorganized with her personal belongings, leaving her clothes, makeup, and jewelry strewn everywhere.

The next film, *The Seven Year Itch* (1955), is the movie in which the most famous costume, the white, pleated halter dress—a must for every serious Marilyn imitator—was featured. Although it has no sequins, feathers, or elaborate beading and is difficult to make because of the pleating, it is definitely worth having because it arouses so much attention and says unmistakably loud and clear, "Hi, I'm Marilyn!" Be sure to wear white panties underneath, though, just in case you have to step over a fan. Marilyn actually wore two pairs to prevent her pubic hair from showing through. Apparently, under the bright spotlights and no doubt unbeknownst to her, she was unsuccessful. Later on, she was said to have begun a painful process of bleaching her pubic hair by herself (salons didn't cover this area back in those days) so it would not show through her other white dresses.

I don't wear this showgirl outfit on stage, but Marilyn wore a similiar costume in Gentlemen Prefer Blondes.

Although four of the last five films Marilyn completed were considered by critics to be her best work, most of the costumes in them would not be appropriate or recognizable enough for impersonators. In *Bus Stop* (1956), Marilyn wears a skimpy, tattered corset and torn fishnet stockings—doesn't sound too good, but she still looked fantastic and it was suitable for the saloon singer she portrayed. In *The Prince and the Showgirl* (1957), she is again arrayed in a white gown. It was a lovely, gathered, formfitting long gown with a flare below the knees and three-quarter-length sleeves. *Some Like It Hot* (1959) is set in the 1920s, so Marilyn's dresses are of the flapper-girl type with beaded fringes. (Although I don't remember flapper girls being quite so curvaceous!) Marilyn was much heavier in this film. Two similar dresses, one black and one white, were sewn onto her, accentuating and all but revealing her larger-than-normal breasts.

"Growing up, people use to tell me that I reminded them of Marilyn Monroe. Yet I preferred to dress in anything from Goth to psychedelic mod and was into early punk rock. When I was fourteen, I was cast as a Marilyn Monroe type in an independent film, and later was cast as an impersonator on a riverboat casino because my acting teacher saw the 'Marilyn' in me. Finally, after being hired several times to do Marilyn at events, I gave in and realized I could actually make a living at it. Now I embrace it and have a wonderful time spreading a little sunshine."

Holly Beavon,
Marilyn Monroe impersonator,
Chicago and L.A.

"My Heart Belongs to Daddy" was the opening number in *Let's Make Love* (1960) and is a great song to perform, but I'm afraid if you showed up to one of your gigs adorned in nothing but black stockings and a sweater, you'd have a little explaining to do. Later on in the film, Marilyn dons a more alluring long, beaded, spaghetti-strapped, fringed white gown, which I would buy immediately if I found it on the rack. Finally, both *The Misfits* (1961) and the unfinished but notorious *Something's Got to Give* (1962) have Marilyn clad in printed, figure-enhancing white dresses just below the knee. Probably not glittery enough for your typical Marilyn stage show, but still radiantly "Marilyn."

I'd like to point out here that, contrary to how I've seen some impersonators portray Marilyn, her most famous costumes showed little or no cleavage. The studio simply wouldn't allow it. By today's standards, the majority of Monroe's costumes showed taste and class. Even those that were controversial, such as the gold lamé or the "Happy Birthday, Mr. President" dress, don't come across in photos and film clips as being vulgar. In other words, when a girl does a take on Marilyn by allowing herself to hang out all over the place, not only is it not an accurate portrayal, but it looks extremely campy and makes a farce of the Monroe image.

My rendition of the gold lamé dress.

Other Unforgettable Attire

A few of Marilyn's most renowned ensembles are not seen in any movie. In May 1962, she joined a host of entertainers at a birthday celebration for President John F. Kennedy. Her rendition of "Happy Birthday"—and the sheer, skintight, beaded gown (by Jean Louis) which she had to be sewn into, along with a white mink coat—has become one of the most notorious moments in Monroe history. This is actually my favorite look to emulate. Although my beaded gown is opaque white and not sheer, I can get into it without help, and, of course, my fur is faux and not mink.

Ten years earlier, when Marilyn was the Grand Marshal of the Miss America Pageant, she wore a black halter dress with a white collar and a plunging neckline that created quite a flurry. She did studio shots in the same dress, and it is from these photos that Andy Warhol created his illustrious renditions of Marilyn. This would be a cute dress to replicate for more casual Marilyn gigs or photo shoots.

Some of the most celebrated photos of Marilyn were taken by Milton Greene. For one of their shoots, the dress Greene had ordered turned out to be too small. Greene told Marilyn just to hold the dress up against her. The result became infamous. These are the photos where Marilyn is sitting barefoot in a dance studio and appears to be wearing a white sheer ballerina dress with crinoline. It just goes to show, Marilyn really could look incredible in—or out of—anything.

Here I am wearing an imitation of the "Happy Birthday, Mr. President" dress by Jean Louis. The original sold in a 1999 Christie's auction in New York for a staggering $1.5 million.

Accessories

"Get high heels and always keep your shoes the same color as your stockings, black with black, nude with nude. It makes you taller, get it?"

Marilyn Monroe to Susan Strasberg

Looking at Marilyn's photos and movies, I'm not sure she always followed her own advice. In *Niagara*, Marilyn's shoes were black heels with black ankle straps while her hose was nude, and in *How to Marry a Millionaire*, posing in a red bathing suit, she wore high platforms with red ankle straps. Her legs looked great regardless. The following is a list of the shoes she wore with her most famous outfits.

Gentlemen Prefer Blondes:
    pink strapless gown—black, patent sling backs
    red sequined gown—red sequined pumps with open toe
    gold lamé gown—strappy open-toe heels in gold
The Seven Year Itch:
    white dress—white sling backs
There's No Business:
    white gown—white sling backs
Performing for the troops in Korea:
    plum-sequined dress—nude heels with ankle strap

Hats, Gloves, and Jewelry

Not many famous photographs show Marilyn wearing hats or headdresses, but she did wear some in her movies and occasionally in her personal life. In fact, she looks fantastic, in a black beret tilted to the side as worn in *Gentlemen Prefer Blondes*, *How to Marry a Millionaire*, and *Niagara*. And, she wore some feathered headdresses in *Gentlemen Prefer Blondes*, *There's No Business Like Show Business*, and *River of No Return*. When not on the job, she sometimes wore a black, bowl-shaped hat to run around in.

Gloves were a must in the 1950s. Marilyn often wore long or elbow-length gloves with her evening dresses and short gloves with her suits and casual dresses.

Diamonds may be a girl's best friend, but in her personal life Marilyn seldom wore real diamonds. She didn't wear much jewelry at all—she felt it detracted from her face. She most often just wore—believe it or not—rhinestone earrings. On the rare occasions when she did wear a necklace, you might see her in a short strand of real pearls given to her by Joe DiMaggio. She also did not like to wear rings because she thought her fingers were fat and she didn't want to call attention to them. However, her screen persona is another story. If you're going to imitate the "Diamonds Are a Girl's Best Friend" look, then you've got to get heavily decked out in rhinestone earrings, chokers, necklaces, and bracelets just as Marilyn did. You're off the hook if you choose to mimic the *Seven Year Itch* look, the "Happy Birthday, Mr. President," or the gold lamé guises, because Marilyn wore only earrings with those ensembles.

Marilyn's Personal Wardrobe

Marilyn's taste in apparel changed throughout the different phases of her life. There was the young Norma Jeane dressed in swimsuits and youthful casual wear. There was the starlet turned Marilyn Monroe decked in sexy halter dresses and evening gowns. Then there was the New York Marilyn—the rebel who broke her contract with 20th Century Fox and disappeared to New York to try to shake her stereotype. The latter is the Marilyn who went head-to-head with the studio bigwigs, putting her career on the line because she wanted, above all things, respect. George Nardiello was called upon by the Greenes to help create a new wardrobe for Marilyn, thereby creating a new image. Marilyn was later to say, however, that Milton Greene had tried to make her into a fashion-model type like his wife, Amy, which, Marilyn said, she was not. And furthermore, though her personal wardrobe may have gained a new sophistication, Marilyn never wavered in her desire to have her clothes a size too small and to show off her notorious curves.

A dress with a slit up the leg is a guaranteed show-stopper.

Lena Pepitone, Marilyn's wardrobe mistress during these latter years in New York (during her marriage to Arthur Miller), described her wardrobe as consisting of identical pairs of black or brown velvet slacks (her pants were mostly fitted, zipped up the side or back, and tapered at the ankle), many identical pairs of black-and-white checkered pants, beige and white cotton and silk blouses, scores of pairs of Ferragamo flats, and an "endless array of spaghetti-strap dresses with plunging necklines, four mink coats, and bottles and bottles of her favorite perfumes, Chanel No. 5 and Joy." Pepitone claims that Marilyn had no underwear at all. Susan Strasberg also said that Marilyn often wore no underwear when they went shopping, and often stripped naked in front of the salesladies. Exactly to what extent you want to parody Marilyn's dressing habits is your business, but she did have a point—panty lines show—especially when your clothes are painted on. But seriously, following Marilyn's wardrobe wouldn't be a bad idea. The look is timeless and the color selections are easy to mix and match—beige, white, black, and brown (beige, white, black, and red were Marilyn's favorite colors)—and spaghetti-strap dresses are a must-have for every aspiring Monroe clone.

Marilyn with actor Tom Ewell in a scene from The Seven Year Itch, *1955.*

Marilyn also had some special getups that she wore on certain occasions. At her acting classes at the Actor's Studio in New York, she often was seen in jeans and a baggy sweater, no makeup, and her bowl hat. When she wanted to be completely unrecognizable, she wore a black wig, a maternity outfit, and low-heeled shoes.

Marilyn idolized intellectuals, particularly Abraham Lincoln, whose picture she kept above her bed. She said that her third husband, playwright Arthur Miller, looked like Lincoln without the beard.

Making the Monroe Look Work for You

Attempting a Monroe replication isn't exactly as simple as it may seem sometimes. When I first started, I imagined myself in Marilyn's place, in the pink gown, mimicking her every move and surrounded by backup dancers in tuxedos who would carry me up and down large staircases on a seemingly endless stage. The reality proved to be much different. I found that the client would request that I wear a certain dress and sing several songs—but often the costume requested wasn't even from the same movie as the song. It was very frustrating. If I was singing "After You Get What You Want, You Don't Want It," I wanted to be wearing a long white gown with a slit up the leg. And if I was singing "Diamonds," I didn't want to be wearing the white dress. I wanted to imitate everything perfectly. But I finally realized that's not possible. So what that means is that you may be able to combine the ideas of several Marilyn dresses into one. In other words, if you have a pink dress with a slit up the leg, that might work great—or if you have a red sequined gown with spaghetti straps instead of long sleeves, you could be in business. That doesn't mean you shouldn't work toward having a few exact replicas made, but it does mean that nothing will ever be exactly like it was in the movies, and it can really work in your favor to have one or two gowns that give you the ability to combine several Marilyn looks into one. You can see exactly what I mean in the photos of some of my gowns.

Don't Cry for Me, Japan...

In the fall of 1995, I flew to Tokyo for the first time to perform in a clothing manufacturers fashion show as a variety act between the modeling numbers. We performed three shows a day, four days in Tokyo and two days in Osaka. The models had many "quick changes" and I had three of my own. So we each had our own dresser/personal assistant, each of whom took her job as seriously as if she were dressing the Queen Mother! Polite and gracious, our Japanese hosts had already treated us many times to exquisite Japanese cuisine and tours of local sights and shrines. But I was still taken by surprise when, after our final performance, our dressers presented us each with gifts—and began crying aloud because our jobs were over and we would soon be leaving!

You may find spin-off costumes (including shoes, gloves, and rhinestone jewelry) at thrift stores or vintage stores—but beware! Your alterations may cost well more than the dress, and those items are not returnable. Believe it or not, I've purchased some wonderful Marilyn-derivative dresses in department stores. Shop during the holidays and you should find an array of sequined gowns. You should also make every effort to choose costumes that are the most flattering to your figure, or rather, make your figure look like Marilyn's. You may need to wear padding underneath, such as a bustier, or if your hips are narrow, a girdle with hip pads (Frederick's of Hollywood sells these). Your waist should be well cinched to accentuate your hips (unless they already speak for themselves).

If you feel overwhelmed by all this, there is an alternative. Many costume shops sell a knockoff of the *Seven Year Itch* white dress, and during Halloween, I've even seen a version of the pink satin *Diamonds* dress. The cost runs between $20 and $30 for the white one, and $70 to $80 for the pink gown, so obviously the quality is not so great. But if your budget is tight, you're not ready to dive in with expensive costumes for your first outing as Marilyn, or this is only a one-time fling as Marilyn, then these offer a good alternative. If you're handy with a sewing machine or have a dressmaker, patterns for both of these dresses are made by Simplicity.

An example of one of my favorite spin-off costumes.

"Marilyn Glamour" for Everyone

Of course, not everyone wants to bleach her hair and become a Marilyn impersonator (thank God, or I'd be out of a job). The gist here is that you can use most of these concepts to transform or enhance your image into a classic, glamorous one.

You can follow the makeup steps in Chapter One, but skip the part where I contour to make my face look like Marilyn's. Use any shade of blush and red lipstick you like (but follow your own lip line). The mole is optional.

As for your hair, whatever the color, *a solid color*—as opposed to highlights or streaks—whether blonde, red, or brunette, will give a more classic, glamorous look, and whatever the length, use a strong gel to push it up and away from the hairline and off of your face. Then use hot rollers. If you're a redhead, you may end up looking like Rita Hayworth or a young Lucille Ball. If you're a brunette, you might find you're an Ava Gardner or Elizabeth Taylor type.

Formfitting (not skintight), classically cut skirts and slacks with feminine but tailored blouses and wide, waist-enhancing belts or sashes will top off the look. If you're a businesswoman, find suits that are tapered at the waist and have skirts tapered down the leg. For evening wear, look for spaghetti-strap, strapless, or halter dresses and gowns with structured bodices and thick fabrics like satin and tapestry weaves (not the flimsy polyester that is prevalent today).

CHAPTER THREE

There's Something

About Marilyn

Capturing the Persona and the Performance

Imitation is the sincerest form of flattery.

What do people want when they hire a Marilyn Monroe impersonator to entertain at their event? Is it the look? The nostalgia? Are they just hoping to see a gust of wind send a girl in a white dress airborne like Mary Poppins? What do they really expect? Marilyn Monroe represented a lot more than just a blonde with red lips and a mole. If that's all they want, they could choose from thousands of models or a cardboard cutout if they're on a budget. Marilyn was a part of a romanticized era of American and Hollywood history. In spite of what may have really been going on, the 1950s (the height of Marilyn's fame) are seen as a more innocent age, a simpler time. Marilyn projected a vulnerable naïveté that was accepting and loving of any and all creatures. She seemed willing to love and accept anyone who would love and accept her back.

This is the dress I wear most often, an imitation of the famous Seven Year Itch *dress.*

Marilyn loved animals and took in several strays while living with husband Arthur Miller in Connecticut.

So what does all this mean? For me it means that, in spite of myself, I have to go to every gig with that same attitude of being open and friendly, making every person feel as special as Marilyn made her public feel. In other words, you don't just stand in a corner and look pretty (although sometimes Marilyn was so shy in public gatherings that that's exactly what she did). You have to go up to every stranger as if he or she is your best friend. And, believe me, this will be easy, because that's what everyone will be doing to you.

So that's the beginning. That's the attitude to start with. From there, it's necessary to build the Marilyn character, including the voice, mannerisms, walk, talk, and performances.

My First Performance

My first performance as Marilyn was at the American Renegade Theatre in North Hollywood, California. I tried to back out at the last minute because I was so scared, but the Frank Sinatra impersonator who had got me started pleaded with me to go on. When I did, I was so blinded by the spotlight, which I was not yet accustomed to, that I started singing "I wanna be loved by you" to someone in the audience who, when I got closer, I realized was a woman! The audience found it amusing and applauded with delight.

Her Characters in Film

You've probably figured out by now that you're going to have to know a lot about Marilyn, including the movies she was in, her costars, what she wore, when the film was made, who the director was, the costume designer, the studio, and other such trivia. You'll also need to know facts and trivia about her real life: where she was born, how she got started, her husbands and boyfriends. For that information, I suggest you read several biographies (consult the reading list at the end of this book). Why do you need to know all of this, you ask? Because you're Marilyn! I know, I know, you're not really her, but the whole fun of it—and the reason impersonators get paid well—is that people want to see and talk to the real Marilyn. Impersonators are the closest they're going to get, so it's necessary to create "suspension of disbelief" (that's the acting term for being so darned good that even though the audience knows something's not real, they're having such a good time with it that they allow themselves to think it's real). People will come up to you and ask you or *tell* you about your (Marilyn's) movies, your life—even your love life. So you have to be prepared to "answer in character" (a phrase that means to be acting like someone else to the point where you feel like you *are* that person—it's not as difficult as it sounds). So let's get started by looking at the movie characters that have shaped our perception of Marilyn Monroe.

Fortunately, this policeman was only giving me directions!

Marilyn was known for being perpetually late. She once kept Laurence Rockefeller waiting for two hours. (Rockefeller later said no one had ever done this before.)

Although she tried hard to shake it later in her career, it was that stereotypical dumb blonde image that Marilyn used to propel her to stardom. That she later proved a serious actress made her legacy a lasting one, but the dumb blonde image still sticks. Many Monroe characters were variations on the dumb blonde persona, but Lorelei Lee from *Gentlemen Prefer Blondes* has become legendary. In fact, I would go so far as to say that *GPB* is the Marilyn bible for impersonators. You must know every one of Marilyn's lines, songs, and expressions from this movie.

The brilliance in Monroe's portrayal of Lorelei Lee is that she isn't really a dumb blonde. She just has an entirely different way of reasoning than most normal people and a very focused agenda—namely to obtain diamonds and marry well. She even says, "I can be smart when it's important, but most men don't like it." Here are some other great lines from the movie.

"She [referring to Jane Russell's character, Dorothy] really needs someone like I to educate her."

"A girl like I almost never gets to meet really interesting men. Sometimes my brain gets real starved."

"Coupons…that's just like money, isn't it?"

"It's just as easy to fall in love with a rich man as a poor man."

"If a girl is spending all of her time worrying about all the money she doesn't have, how is she going to have any time for being in love?"

"I won't let myself fall in love with a man who won't trust me no matter what I might do." (I love this one!)

"Thank you ever so."

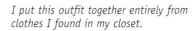

I put this outfit together entirely from clothes I found in my closet.

You may find other amusing lines in the movie, but these are among my favorites, and I find them easy to incorporate into my dialogue. You can also create your own banter based on these ideas. Basically, Lorelei tried to speak as though she were educated but usually ended up misusing or mispronouncing words. She also does this in *Monkey Business* when she says that her boss was complaining about her punctuation so she now tries to get to work early. In your conversations with people while you're Marilyn, try to pick up on certain words they say and turn them into something entirely different. You can often get several minutes of entertaining banter going on. For example, if someone tells me they're a vice president of the company, I might respond by saying something like, "That's OK, most presidents have vices. I have some vices myself," or, "'I wouldn't say that too loudly, you might get in trouble. Pretty soon the press will be here wanting to know exactly what vice you have." People usually take the ball and run with it at that point. But you've got to say everything in that innocent, naive Lorelei Lee voice or it won't be funny (trust me on this).

Another classic Monroe character was the girl upstairs (she had no name) in *The Seven Year Itch*. Still the naive and innocent one, Marilyn plays the beautiful tease who doesn't seem to realize the effect she has on men, and is unpretentious and unaware of her own striking beauty. (The latter quality is why female audiences were not intimidated by Marilyn, and as most of the crowds you'll be working with are full of women, it's important that you project this wonderful quality.) Marilyn isn't playing the gold digger in this picture. Rather she makes a middle-aged man of average appearance feel special again. I hate to admit it, but that last

sentence could practically be the job description for Marilyn impersonators. Seriously though, in her innocuous tone, the girl upstairs says things like:

"[When it's hot like this] I keep my undies in the icebox."

"A married man, air-conditioning, champagne, and potato chips! It's just a wonderful party!"

"I think you're just elegant!"

"Oh, do you feel the breeze from the subway? Isn't it delicious!"

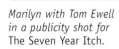

Marilyn with Tom Ewell in a publicity shot for The Seven Year Itch.

Keep in mind that when you wear *The Seven Year Itch* white dress from the subway scene, you're going to get a lot of questions like, "Hey, Marilyn, where's the air to blow up your skirt?" or "Where's the fan?" I sometimes answer, "I didn't bring my fan. They told me there were going to be plenty of wind bags at this party already!"

In *How to Marry a Millionaire*, Marilyn plays Pola, a model who won't wear her glasses because she's afraid men won't be attracted to her, and she is again plotting to marry a millionaire. She does some slapstick here, like running into walls, following the wrong man in the restaurant, reading a book upside down, and taking a plane to Kansas City instead of Atlantic City. (If you have a pair of 1950s-style glasses with rhinestones, you could have a ball with this. Accidentally run into someone, then pull out your glasses and exclaim, "Why you're just like a man, aren't you?" This could be a great way of breaking into a crowd and getting conversation going.)

Pola also has a few good dizzy-blonde lines. When someone is talking about cattle, she exclaims brilliantly, "You know, like cows." When David Wayne tells her she's reading the book upside down, she denies that she is upside down.

> "One day when I was at Universal Studios posing for photos, a woman from India saw me. Her jaw dropped and she was frozen for a second and started shaking. She mumbled something in her native tongue and said 'Marilyn Monroe' and then she fainted. I had someone call first aid, but by the time the nurse arrived, the woman was already up having her photo taken with me."
>
> Dena Drotar,
> Marilyn Monroe
> impersonator,
> Los Angeles

Marilyn was an insomniac. She would read until all hours of the morning and often called her friends as late as 3 and 4 A.M.

Marilyn has a thing for saxophone players in *Some Like It Hot* and once again she is searching for millionaires, but deep down, we know all she really wants is love. This is probably Monroe's most highly acclaimed film, and her ability as a comedienne was fully realized. Some of her best lines:

"I can quit drinking any time I want to, only I don't want to."

"I'm tired of getting the fuzzy end of the lollipop."

[In answer to the question, "What's in Florida?"] "Millionaires! Tons of 'em. They flock there in the winter like birds!"

Posing with Tony Curtis and Jack Lemmon look-alikes "Daphne" and "Josephine" at a Some Like it Hot *party at the Hotel del Coronado, where the movie was filmed.*

Marilyn has one of her longest monologues in film during one scene on the train with Tony Curtis where she is telling him about her past. This is something that I have memorized in case I need to give a monologue as Marilyn at an audition. At mix-and-mingle events, I use bits and pieces of it here and there, sometimes changing the words to suit the occasion.

Gentlemen Prefer Blondes, The Seven Year Itch, How to Marry a Millionaire, and *Some Like It Hot*—these are what I call the fab four films that capture the comedic side of Monroe as well as contain some of her best dialogue. (But watch all of her movies yourself and draw your own conclusions and your own interpretation of Marilyn.)

Marilyn with Jane Russell in Gentlemen Prefer Blondes *(1953)*

Voice and Vocals

"It isn't necessary to use your voice in any special way [to sound sexy]. If you think something sexy, the voice just naturally goes along."

Marilyn Monroe

Marilyn said this in one of her final interviews. By then she had mastered the sexy voice and changed it subtly to suit the different characters she portrayed. But now that you have an idea of what you're going to say and the emotions to express when you say it, how do you imitate Marilyn's voice? When she was just an aspiring starlet, her voice was described by some, including Shelley Winters, as a "high-pitched squeak." As usual, many people take credit for helping Marilyn to lower her voice, including Natasha Lytess, Freddy Karger, Hal Shaeffer, Billie Daniels, Phil Moore, Ken Darby, and even choreographer Jack Cole. No doubt they all contributed, with Freddy Karger and Hal Shaeffer teaching her to sing also.

Margaret Mclean helped with her speech. Marilyn's voice and enunciation were slightly different from film to film. She overexaggerated her mouth movements in *Gentlemen Prefer Blondes*, *How to Marry a Millionaire*, and *The Seven Year Itch* more than in her other films. For the most part, as an impersonator, it is sometimes best to do the most extreme side of the persona. That creates a more stereotypical and easily recognizable character. But if you overdo it, you risk becoming a farce. As we'll discuss later, you'll need to videotape yourself and get feedback from others to see how you're coming across.

Marilyn's singing voice was sometimes breathy and soft like her speaking voice. But she also had a very quick vibrato that made her voice distinctive, and it became more exaggerated with time. Compare her vocal delivery in the songs from *Ladies of the Chorus* with that of *Let's Make Love*. The style and

Some said that Marilyn's mouth was her best feature.

interpretation in the latter are, of course, more confident and brazenly sexy, but the vibrato is also much more pronounced. Marilyn's rendition of "Happy Birthday, Mr. President" is more true to her youthful self; only her breathlessness was more evident. Other distinctions include her enunciation. She had a way of holding onto a word and a note just a fraction longer than the rhythm intended. This didn't take her off rhythm, though. It was just the sensual way she had of milking every word that came out of her mouth for everything it was worth.

River of No Return saw Marilyn singing some serious ballads in the lower registers of her voice, while in *Some Like It Hot*'s "I Wanna Be Loved by You" and "Runnin' Wild"; her voice was higher pitched and more little girlish. One of Marilyn's key influences as a singer was Ella Fitzgerald. When she first began taking vocal lessons, Marilyn was told to listen to and emulate Ella.

You may need to take voice lessons to learn to sing like Marilyn or even to learn how to sing. If you do, don't feel bad. After all, Marilyn took many voice lessons. Personally, I think that, lessons or no lessons, you're going to have to spend a lot of time listening to, and singing along with, Marilyn's songs. You may be able to find CDs or cassettes of Marilyn's recordings in the music store. Otherwise, you can record them from your VCR to your tape deck. Practice until you no longer hear a difference between Marilyn's voice and yours.

When re-creating the Marilyn look, it helps to make use of every part of your body.

Poise, Posture, and Poses

"How did a high school dropout, victim of eleven foster homes, learn the poise and posture we see in every photograph?"

Michael Ventura, *Marilyn Monroe from Beginning to End*

Arthur Miller called Marilyn the most "womanly woman" he'd ever known. Alexandra Heilweil, the child actress who played her daughter in *Something's Got to Give*, said of Marilyn, "…To this day she's the model that I have of femininity…it was her poise really, not so much her face and figure, that made her so beautiful…the way she carried herself and the way she moved and spoke was utterly feminine."

Many others noted Marilyn's complete and utter femininity, and it is this feminine, delicate, poised manner in which we always see her. Her posture was impeccable. She seemed completely aware of her body at all times— shoulders back, head high, chest up, one leg posed slightly in front of the other—and yet it was second nature to her. Being a tomboy myself, I feel exhausted after only a few hours of such feminine posturing and posing. The second I get home, my shoes, jewelry, and wig are strewn in a trail behind me and I'm soon slouching in a chair in front of the television, cracking open a beer. Sorry, Mom. I can't quite picture Marilyn doing the same. Her femininity was not an act, and although she practiced her poses in front of the mirror for hours and knew every angle of her body and what was most flattering, when she was caught off guard, her poise was just as present. The truth is that the

Posing for the camera at a charity ball.

way Marilyn carried herself is a dying art. In spite of what our mothers and grandmothers told us ("Straighten up! Shoulders back!"), popular culture tells us otherwise. Photo and runway models today project the hipper, grungier, unisex, Generation X attitude. This only serves to make Marilyn's image shine even brighter by contrast.

Wiggle, Walk, Wink, and Wave

"I started when I was six months old and haven't stopped since."

Marilyn Monroe, when asked about her walk

More has been made of Marilyn's sexy amble than that of any other star in history. Her walk away from the camera in *Niagara* was the longest in film history. How she created that special wiggle has been the subject of a great deal of speculation. Some say she cut one heel one-quarter inch shorter than the other. Emmiline Snively said that Marilyn had weak ankles. Donald Spoto said that the cobblestone street in *Niagara* threw Marilyn's gait into the "seductive swivel she used forever after." Ralph Roberts, her masseur, claimed it was the result of an exercise she did where she moved from one buttock to another while sitting. Choreographer Jack Cole, acting coach Natasha Lytess, and a host of others take credit for helping Marilyn create her seductive stride. I have found that wearing a very tight dress that allows for little leg movement, coupled with taking short steps and placing one foot in front of the other as if walking a fine line (a concept I'm all too familiar with), helps me to achieve a hip gyration somewhere between subtle and potentially harmful to passersby.

Practicing the Marilyn strut.

The most often run clip of Marilyn's playful wink is from the finale of the song "My Heart Belongs to Daddy" from the film *Let's Make Love*. Study this wink, which was precluded by a kiss, and incorporate it into your repertoire of Monroe gestures. The Marilyn wave is also not to be overlooked. Even that was unique. So many photographs and film clips show her warmly waving to her fans and blowing kisses as well. There's a famous scene in *The Seven Year Itch* where Marilyn, perched out of the second-floor window of her apartment wearing the notorious white terry-cloth robe, is waving good-bye to Tom Ewell. She twists her wrists back and forth instead of just waving her hand from side to side like most people. It comes across as a demure, gentle, feminine gesture, like everything else she did.

Marilyn's Marriages

Marilyn had three husbands in her life and possibly four. The first marriage was to James Dougherty in 1942, when Marilyn was just sixteen. Their marriage lasted four years. The second, briefest (nine months), and most notorious was to the late baseball great Joe DiMaggio in 1954. Third, in 1956, was to playwright Arthur Miller (*Death of a Salesman*, *The Crucible*), also lasting four years. Robert Slatzer, a longtime friend and sometimes lover of Marilyn, claims they were married in Mexico but that studio heads made Marilyn have the marriage annulled a few days later.

A white dress is always a glamorous choice.

It is rumored that Marilyn was offered the opportunity to marry Prince Rainier and become the Princess of Monaco.

Provocative Performances

It was that cinematic musical masterpiece "Diamonds Are a Girl's Best Friend" that first put a longing in me to be that beautiful doll dressed in pink satin and diamonds. Apparently, I was not alone in my desire to mirror that image, as Madonna imitated the costume and set design exactly in her "Material Girl" video. Madonna used her own personality and voice, however. Mira Sorvino attempted to duplicate the number when she portrayed Marilyn in the HBO movie *Norma Jean and Marilyn*.

Marilyn's scene was choreographed by Jack Cole, who worked with her on most of her musical numbers throughout her career. She had studied dance while a starlet at the studio, but a dancer in the true sense of the word she was not. In *Ladies of the Chorus*, her movements were kept very simple and her arms were sometimes stiff. *Gentlemen Prefer Blondes* was her first musical since *Ladies*, and her progress was amazing. Jane Russell reported that Marilyn would stay hours later than her to have Jack go over and over the routines. Cole was very patient with Marilyn, and his brilliant choreography made Monroe and Russell's simple, small movements seem grandiose. "Two Little Girls from Little Rock" and "When Love Goes Wrong" are classic numbers choreographed to make the most of the costumes, set, and the leading ladies. When you break down Marilyn's steps and movements in these numbers as I have with my friend and choreographer Heidi Anderson (who also worked with Bridget Fonda in her role as a Marilyn impersonator in the David Winkler film *Finding Graceland*), you will find that the

Live and in character.

movements are small and sometimes awkward. The key is to make every tiny gesture meaningful and sensual, as Marilyn did. However, you'll need to change some of the moves to suit a live stage show *without* props or backup dancers, because you won't often be performing on an elaborate soundstage in a multimillion-dollar production!

Cole also choreographed Marilyn in *There's No Business Like Show Business*, where she performed "After You Get What You Want You Don't Want It" and "Heatwave." The former is probably her most sensational solo number. No dancers, just Marilyn alone working a stage and a crowd to the hilt. Her poise, presence, and energy from her entrance to her exit are dazzling. Again the movements are simple and take advantage of the high slit up the leg of her gown, but she takes even the slightest motion and performs it to its maximum potential. Monroe had such confidence in Cole that she called upon him for help even in films where he had not been hired as the choreographer, such as *Some Like It Hot* and *River of No Return*.

"*Pizza*" *Marilyn*...

Wolfgang Puck, the chef who created the pizza delicacies found in the restaurant Spago's in L.A. and, of course, Wolfgang Puck's, was giving a cooking demonstration at a department store in Los Angeles. I was hired to model the "pizza dress" inspired by a piece of Monroe artwork at the Wolfgang Puck restaurant at Universal Studios. Well, I modeled the pizza dress, but I also had to create and sing a new version of "Diamonds Are a Girl's Best Friend." You guessed it— "Pizza Is a Girl's Best Friend." "A burger from McDonald's may be quite continental, but pizza is a girl's best friend" ...Mama mia!

As far as some of her most common mannerisms and motions, there are a few that stand out as classic Monroe moves. It's too simplistic to say that she just shook her hips and wiggled her shoulders. With the exception of "Heatwave," most of her shoulder shrugs or hip gyrations were subtle. A shrug of the shoulders might be accompanied by a playful wrinkle of the nose; a bump with the hips would likely be toned down with a gleaming, childlike, open-mouthed smile. Arms spread wide or stretched high above the head, hands placed delicately on the upper chest, an enthusiastic strut with arms swinging back and forth—these are just a few bits of Marilyn choreography. It's difficult to describe or demonstrate here, so I strongly recommend you find a dance instructor or even a trained dancer (probably less expensive than an instructor) who can watch Marilyn's videos and teach you the basics. You may only need a few sessions to get you on the right track, and the money you spend (from $10 to $35 per hour and up) will pay for itself in the knowledge and confidence you will gain. You'll be on your own as far as the nose wiggle is concerned, though.

Feminine hand poses are an important Marilyn mannerism.

Marilyn's Public and Private Personas

"I'm close, I can feel it, I can hear it, but it isn't really me."

Marilyn Monroe, on her image

Marilyn never wanted to let her public down, and at movie premieres and special appearances, she maintained her sexy, glamorous, adoring image. Privately, however, she had begun to resent the very dumb blonde image that had brought her to fame. She wanted desperately to become a "serious actress" and to educate herself. A high school dropout, she began to immerse herself in great literary works and poetry. She learned as much as she could about politics, history, and the world around her. She was smart and courageous enough to risk her career by leaving Hollywood and forming Marilyn Monroe Productions in New York with Milton Greene in 1955. Her renegotiated contract gave her the right to choose which scripts and directors she would work with plus a $100,000 per-picture salary that had all of Hollywood talking. The studio heads were on *their* knees this time. They didn't understand that this woman wasn't satisfied with only stardom and glamour. She wasn't motivated by money. She just "wanted to be wonderful." Marilyn didn't want people to laugh at her, and she wanted to be taken seriously. She realized her goals with the critically acclaimed *Bus Stop*, *Some Like It Hot*, and *The Misfits*, and with millions of fans all over the world who find her wonderful and take her seriously to a greater extent than she will ever know.

No, I'm not reading Chekhov. Just give me a good mystery.

BeMarilyn!

CHAPTER FOUR

The Live Performance

Marilyn on Stage

"She had a luminous quality—a combination of wistfulness, radiance, yearning—to set her apart and yet make everyone wish to be part of it, to share in the childish naïveté which was at once so shy and yet so vibrant. This quality was even more evident when she was on the stage….Without a doubt she would have been one of the really great actresses of the stage."

Lee Strasberg, at Marilyn's funeral

A Broadway baby Marilyn wasn't; nonetheless, the screen goddess did have stage experience. Before she became a star, she joined a theater group at the Bliss-Hayden Playhouse in Beverly Hills. She performed in several plays, including *Glamour Preferred*, a revival of Florence Ryerson and Colin Clements' 1940 Broadway play in which she had the second lead and played, fittingly, a screen siren. She reportedly had roles in other plays in the theater, although there are no known reviews of them. In 1955, she went to study acting in New York with Lee Strasberg. After observing the class for a year, she performed in a scene from Eugene O'Neill's *Anna Kristie* in front of the class. She was excellent by all accounts.

Posing like Marilyn isn't always comfortable, but it should look like it is!

Marilyn the Entertainer

Marilyn's name never lit up the marquee as an entertainer in Las Vegas, but one of her finest moments, by her own admission, came when she went to entertain American troops in Korea. She had been honeymooning in Japan with then-husband Joe DiMaggio when duty called. Marilyn accepted gladly and made the most out of the four-day tour. She wasn't particularly fond of flying, but as the helicopter neared her first stop, she instructed the pilot to get as low to the ground as possible. She then lowered herself out the sliding

door, and with two soldiers holding onto her legs, she waved and blew kisses to the troops. They of course went wild. She had the pilot make several passes. (Fortunately, Marilyn impersonators are not expected to perform such daredevil feats today!)

During the course of her tour, Marilyn performed ten live shows in front of more than 100,000 troops. She sang songs like "Diamonds Are a Girl's Best Friend," "Do It Again" (the lyrics of which had to be changed to "Kiss Me Again" to avoid being too suggestive), "Somebody Love Me," and "Bye Bye Baby." She wore a sequined, spaghetti-strap, calf-length, plum-colored dress in spite of the freezing temperatures. During one of her songs, Marilyn walked over to a soldier who was trying to take her picture. She reached down, took off the lens cover, and said, "You forgot to take it off, honey." The troops roared with approval. Riots nearly broke out during several of her performances, with soldiers rushing the stage to the point where Marilyn had to stop her act and back away from the microphone until they settled down. At another performance, a soldier was trampled and had to be rushed to the infirmary.

For her heroic effort to boost the morale of the American troops, Marilyn was given a helmet by the 25th Division, an honorary scroll by the military police, and adulation like she had never before experienced. She also contracted a mild case of pneumonia, but never complained, and recovered in a hospital back in Japan.

Imitating one of Marilyn's most famous poses.

Other Public Appearances

Such is the gratification of live performance. It probably explains why Marilyn enjoyed going out in public as much as she did. As a young starlet working for the studios, she made many public appearances at restaurant openings, parades, and awards ceremonies. (Marilyn presented a new house as an award to the winner of a contest for *Photoplay* magazine, and she presented the Oscar for Sound Achievement to Thomas T. Moulton for *All About Eve*—it was her only appearance at the Academy Awards.) She was sent out as a starlet caddie at a Cheviot Hills golf benefit in Los Angeles. And of course, she posed for hundreds of magazines, papers, catalogs, and the infamous "Golden Dreams" calendar where she posed nude against a red velvet background.

For a television performance in Bogota, Columbia, I was provided with these handsome back-up dancers.

Marilyn made $50 for posing in the nude for the infamous

"Golden Dreams" calendar shot in 1949 when she was a struggling starlet. It is estimated that

the photo later generated over $750,000 in revenue for its owner, John Baumgarth.

Even as a full-fledged star, Marilyn continued to make special appearances. In addition to being the Grand Marshal in a parade for the Miss America Pageant, she sang a song with Jane Russell at the Hollywood Bowl for a benefit for underprivileged children in an event coordinated by Danny Thomas. She was an usherette at the premieres of *East of Eden* and *The Rose Tattoo,* the latter of which raised $100,000 for the Actor's Studio. She was quite fond of charity events and fund-raisers. She visited children's hospitals and orphanages, participated in events such as fashion shows for the March of Dimes, and made a dazzling appearance at Mike Todd's 1955 circus benefit at Madison Square Garden for the Arthritis and Rheumatism Foundation. Dressed in a black corset and fishnet stockings, she rode around the ring astride a pink elephant. (This much photographed scene was imitated by Madonna in one of her many promotional photos.) Supposedly, the costume had been prepared at the last minute because the one actually ordered for the event came in the wrong size, and the costumer had left a pin in the bottom that poked Marilyn and was very painful during her entire ride. But like the pro she was, she kept smiling and waving, and no one ever knew.

Posing with a James Dean look-alike at a classic car show.

"Happy Birthday, Mr. President"

In May 1962, Marilyn gave perhaps her most famous public performance when she sang "Happy Birthday" to President John F. Kennedy at Madison Square Garden. She wasn't the only star at the president's party—other Hollywood legends were there, including Jack Benny, Judy Garland, Ella Fitzgerald, Henry Fonda, and Peggy Lee. But seldom is any footage seen other than that of Marilyn. She prepared for the occasion well in advance by commissioning a special dress to be made by designer Jean Louis. She told her studio that she would be going to the party and left the set of *Something's Got to Give* early. Studio executives were furious, but long after Marilyn's death they realized they had failed to capitalize on a publicity stunt that most studios could only dream of. On that night, Marilyn sang "Happy Birthday" a cappella and "Thanks, Mr. President" to the tune of "Thanks for the Memories," the lyrics of which had been changed to the following:

Thanks, Mr. President,

For all the things you've done.

The battles that you've won.

The way you deal with U.S. Steel and our
   problems by the ton.

We thank you, so much...

After that, she led the crowd in singing "Happy Birthday."

Marilyn was extremely nervous about this honor, but wouldn't have missed it for the world. The producer for that evening's gala, Richard Adler, however, had advised the president that the rehearsal with Marilyn singing "Happy Birthday" had not gone well, as she kept bungling the words (so take heart if you're nervous about your first performances). But President Kennedy laughed and said, "Oh, I think she'll be very good." Marilyn had several drinks and was drunk when she was practically pushed onto the stage. (Don't imitate this, Monroe impersonators!) She took time to collect herself, looking out into the crowd and taking deep breaths. She couldn't hear her first note to start the song, and leaned over slightly as the piano player banged the key several times. Finally, she began. Once she did, she made it through with no mistakes. When Marilyn concluded her performance, the president came to the podium and said, "I can now retire from politics after having had 'Happy Birthday' sung to me in such a sweet, wholesome way." A rather underhanded compliment for poor Marilyn.

In Los Angeles at Dodger Stadium on June 1, 1962, Marilyn made an appearance at an Angels baseball game to benefit muscular dystrophy. Wearing a fur-trimmed, light-colored suit and a pillbox hat (the costume was straight from *Something's Got to Give*, which she had been filming that day), and her usual enthusiastic smile, she was escorted onto the field by one of the players. Sadly, this was the last time Marilyn would appear before her adoring public. She died a little over two months later on August 5, 1962.

For the quintessential Marilyn look, I keep my eyes half-closed.

Marilyn became an avid reader in an effort to better herself intellectually. She read the works of Thomas Wolfe, James Joyce, and Ralph Waldo Emerson, to name a few.

It's Showtime!

"I want to be on the stage one day. Chaplin was a magnificent actor. Everything he does is life itself."

Marilyn Monroe to Jack Carroll

If you want to know how Judy Garland, Dolly Parton, or Madonna have acted, sung, and danced on stage—or how they interacted with their audience and what lighting they used—it's easy to find videotapes of their performances. But for Marilyn, it's not quite as easy. You have to study her films, see what will transfer well to the stage, and create your own interpretation of what she would've done in concert. There isn't much footage of her performances with the troops, and those shows were pretty bare bones without much lighting and only a corded microphone (cordless microphones are used today as much as possible to increase freedom of movement). Plus, audiences today require a little more of a show, and face it, impersonators ain't the real thing.

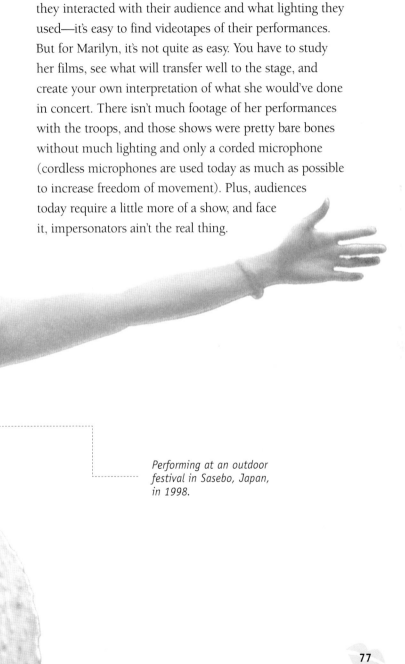

Performing at an outdoor festival in Sasebo, Japan, in 1998.

The good news is that as an impersonator, you have a lot of freedom to interpret Marilyn as you see her or as you think others should see her. One Marilyn impersonator, Katie Labourdette, wrote a stage play based on Marilyn's own words and performed it in theaters around the country. As a singer, I enjoy singing Marilyn's songs and have performed a few one-hour shows singing nearly all of her songs. However, the vast majority of jobs for Marilyn impersonators require a well-honed fifteen- to twenty-minute routine that will be a part of a show with other impersonators. For the last three years, I have been performing such a routine in the critically acclaimed "Hollywood Stars" (producer Ron Stein). We have performed in many showrooms in the United States, including Caesar's Palace, Bally's, Player's Island, the Mirage, and the Chinook Winds Casinos. We have also gone on tour three times in Japan. In this show, I open up with "I Wanna Be Loved by You," in which I include comedic dialogue (see Chapter Three) with a few audience members. Then I sing "My Heart Belongs to Daddy" and bring an audience member (male, of course) on stage and do a comedic routine wherein I mess up his hair and put lip prints on his face while his friends and family members in the audience cheer with delight. My third number is the showstopper "Diamonds Are a Girl's Best Friend." I then do a quick costume change into the white dress while the band is "vamping" and close the set with a short medley of "Some Like It Hot" and "Runnin' Wild." On the final note of "Runnin' Wild," a fan blows my dress as in the subway scene from *The Seven Year Itch.*

Singing for a corporate event in Los Angeles, 1996.

However you (or the producer of your show) choose to construct your act, it should include the following elements:

- popular Marilyn songs, including a very recognizable one for the opening;
- dialogue, preferably funny, with at least one audience member, or to the audience in general;
- audience participation—perhaps bringing someone on stage;
- smooth transitions between numbers (if the music isn't playing, you had better be talking, so there is no uncomfortable "dead air");
- and a strong, upbeat closing number.

There is no right or wrong way to do it as long as you're ultimately basing everything on the real Marilyn and as long as your show fits you. The first thing you need to do is listen to all of Marilyn's songs and decide which ones you can and want to sing.

Here is a list of most of the songs Marilyn either performed in her movies or recorded on albums:

"Diamonds Are a Girl's Best Friend"*

"I Wanna Be Loved by You"*

"My Heart Belongs to Daddy"*

"A Little Girl from Little Rock"*

"Bye Bye Baby"*

"When Love Goes Wrong, Nothing Goes Right"

"After You Get What You Want, You Don't Want It"

"Heat Wave"*

"Lazy"

"Anyone Can See I Love You"

"Like a Woman Should"

"You'd be Surprised"*

"Every Baby Needs a Da-Da-Daddy"

"I'm Gonna File My Claim"*

"Down in the Meadow"

"One Silver Dollar"

"A Fine Romance"

"Do It Again"*

"Kiss"

"Specialization"

"Some Like It Hot"*

"Runnin' Wild"*

"I'm Through with Love"

"That Old Black Magic"

"Happy Birthday"*

"Thanks, Mr. President"

*These are the songs that I have personally performed in my own act.

Once you listen to these songs, consider which ones are the most recognized by the audience and which ones will hold their attention. "Diamonds Are a Girl's Best Friend," "I Wanna Be Loved by You," and "Happy Birthday" are, I believe, the three songs most associated with Marilyn and the ones that I hear mentioned over and over again by clients and people in general when Marilyn is mentioned. Then create a fifteen-minute routine trying to include some Marilynesque dialogue (as taken from her movies as discussed in Chapter Three) either between songs or in the bridge of a song while background music is playing.

You will have to be prepared to sing along to "tracks" (background tapes) as well as bands. As for obtaining the background music for the songs, you're in luck. Most karaoke stores sell a tape or CD by Pocket Songs ($12-$20) with the Marilyn Monroe songs "Diamonds," "Daddy," "Little Girl from Little Rock," "Do It Again," "Bye Bye Baby," and "Heat Wave" (the "Heat Wave" version on this tape is the only song whose arrangement is different

than Marilyn's—all the others sound fairly authentic). At a much greater cost ($250-$350 per song), you can have your songs made to your specifications in a studio. But make sure their preprogrammed instrumentation sounds authentic—most does not. On the occasions when the client you are working for hires a band to accompany you, you will need instrumental charts (sheet music) for your songs, written out by a musician who specializes in this. Instrumentation for a six-piece band shouldn't cost more than $150 to $200 per song. It is important to have easy-to-read, professional charts that have your Marilyn music written exactly as you perform it. That way, even if you have to work with a band in another city or overseas, your show will be consistent.

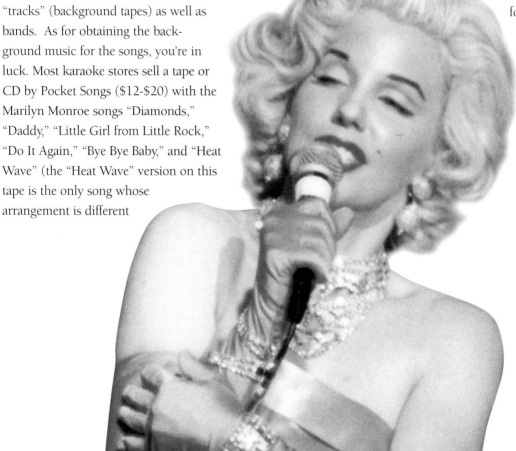

"My Show Belongs to Daddy"

Bringing an audience member on stage is probably the most difficult part of doing a Marilyn stage show, because it brings an unknown element into play. You have to be able to control any situation and try to choose an audience member who looks like they would be a good subject. Sometimes, however, there are certain things you can't foresee. For example, at one show, I had selected a cute, docile elderly man as my prey, but when I took his hand to bring him on stage, although his facial expression said willing, his body was like deadweight. Apparently his entire leg had fallen asleep (he told me this after the show), and I practically had to drag him up the stairs onto the stage. Then there was the shy, conservative, gentle old man who turned out to be an octopus. And I'll never forget the occasion when I brought a man on stage who refused to sit in the "Daddy" chair.

He seemed to want to dance with me or something, but it's not wise to let the audience member take control. So I was trying to corner him and he was trying to corner me. We were squaring off like two wrestlers in an all-star wrestling match. He seemed to just want to dance, so I decided to allow it. But when I got near him, he grabbed me and picked me up, and then gave a triumphant look to the crowd. I was half expecting him to body-slam me and then run around the stage beating his chest! Fortunately, however, I squirmed away and, with a disapproving smile, escorted him off the stage. (I salvaged the number simply saying what I usually say—"Let's give Daddy a big hand, ladies and gentlemen!"—and then finished the last few bars of the song—alone!)

Audience members are usually more than willing to participate.

Most of the time, however, the audience participation is the highlight of the act and draws laughter and applause as the crowd watches a family member, a friend, a colleague, or even their boss, disheveled, grinning from ear to ear, with a red lip print on his cheek. Just how physical you want to become is up to you. I suggest you work up a routine where you move around the audience member, maybe putting his arm around your waist or using a feather or fur boa to wrap around him. In other words, I personally feel that it's best to try to have as little physical contact as possible but make it seem like you're doing a lot. Some Monroe impersonators choose someone with glasses and put lip prints on the glasses and not actually on the "Daddy's" face. Now I'll contradict myself and confess that I sometimes eliminate the "Daddy" routine altogether and keep my audience participation part as simple as going to a few guys in the audience and singing or talking to them where they are.

"On one occasion, during my 'Daddy' routine with Legends in Concert, I brought a blind man on stage (of course, I didn't realize it at first). I kept saying, 'Follow me, Daddy.' But by the time we got on stage it became apparent to me and the audience, because he kept reaching out his arms trying to find me. At the end of the show, I apologized to him and his wife profusely, but they were delighted and bought all the pictures the photographer had taken during the number."

Susan Griffiths,
Marilyn Monroe impersonator,
Tustin, California

Types of Gigs

One of the great things about being an impersonator is getting to experience a variety of venues, clients, and types of jobs. Like the real Marilyn, an impersonator will do grand openings of restaurants, stores, theaters, and other types of businesses, in addition to charity events, award ceremonies, modeling, and of course, birthday parties. There really is no limit to where a gig may be or what type of event or kind of client one may have. I have performed my act or made appearances at trade shows, museums, art galleries, city and county fairs, festivals of all kinds, department store promotional events, shopping mall anniversaries, company picnics, corporate parties and award ceremonies, professional baseball games, jewelry store exhibitions, libraries, casino showrooms, theaters, cruise ships, and hotels. I also had the honor of performing for the American military bases in Okinawa and Sasebo, Japan.

Unfortunately, at classic car shows I never seem to get to drive.

Many of these events do not require a stage show, but just an appearance as Marilyn to meet and greet guests and mingle with them. This requires a different kind of preparation than a stage show. This is where it is important to know your Marilyn trivia, to be prepared to respond to probing but playful questions about the Kennedys such as, "Who was better, Jack or Bobby?" It's hard to believe that people ask these questions, but they do and sometimes it is embarrassing. I have responded by saying things like, "Those were just vicious rumors—we were only friends," or "Well, I think *Jack* Nicholson was excellent in *As Good as It Gets* but *Bobby* De Niro is a great actor, too." People also ask, "'Is your mole real?" or "Is that really your hair?"—and if nobody's asking you the questions, you must be able to approach *them* and start a conversation. You might go up to a group of people and say, "Pardon please, can anyone point me in the direction of the nearest millionaire?" Someone in the group will usually point to one of their friends and giggle, and you've broken the ice and can go from there. It also helps to know what company the guests are with or where they're from, so you can create conversation based on that. Honestly, these "mix and mingle" gigs, as they're commonly called, can be more challenging than a stage show simply because you're always dealing with new people and have to be able to improvise and adapt to the situation. Taking a few acting classes that focus on improvisation would be of great help. Marilyn herself studied acting, mime, dance, and voice.

Planes, Trains, and Automobiles...

By now a veteran of performing in Japan, or so I thought, I had my work cut out for me when I embarked on a taxing, one-month tour in March of '97 in a Stars of Vegas show with Elvis and Michael Jackson impersonators. We had been sent our show schedule in advance, showing the names of the showrooms or clubs we were to perform in each day. What we didn't realize was that the names of the "showrooms" were actually the names of the different cities we would be traveling to. Needless to say, every day or every other day we were packing our bags, running to catch a plane, train, subway, bus, or car, heading to the next "city," performing two shows, sleeping for a few hours, and then getting up to do the same thing all over again. The great part about it was that we went everywhere from the farthest northern cities—the winter wonderlands of Sopporo and Hirosake bordering the Soviet Union—to the beautiful southern city of Beppu, a hot springs mecca for tourists from all over Asia.

From the Spotlight to the Limelight

"The day I returned to Mr. Huston's office for the reading [for The Asphalt Jungle*], I was so nervous. My throat was dry. I had a headache and felt I'd never remember my lines."*

Marilyn Monroe to George Barris, photojournalist

Film, commercial, television, and video work also offer job opportunities for Marilyn Monroe impersonators. Many movies, television shows, commercials, and music videos call for someone to portray Marilyn herself or a Monroe type. If those roles go over the breakdowns (that is, if the producers or casting directors don't already have someone in mind for the part, they put out a casting call to talent agencies), then the agency calls its actresses able to impersonate Marilyn to audition for the roles. Auditioning for these roles can be nerve-racking. In such situations, I've had to read prewritten dialogue, record the audition on videotape at home or in a studio, and then submit it, or just go in and improvise as Marilyn for one to two minutes in front of the casting director. These jobs can be lucrative and exciting. You never know who you might get to work with.

At some of the jobs I've taken part in, I've had the good fortune of meeting or working with people such as Debbie Reynolds, Yasmine Bleeth, the Rembrandts, Hugh Hefner, Ed Begley Jr., Jeff Conoway, Ben E. King, Jeannie Carmen, Bridget Fonda, and Shirley MacLaine.

Here I model a necklace valued at over $1.2 million. Security guards were close by during this "Nature of Diamonds" exhibit in San Diego.

Traveling Overseas

"I like getting there, not the actual traveling itself. I've never been to Italy, but I love Italians. Paris I hear is a marvelous place too—the City of Lights. It must be beautiful; I hope someday to go there and all these other exciting places. I've traveled to England, Korea, Japan, and Mexico. I've been to Canada, too—Canadian Rockies and Banff."

Marilyn Monroe in her last interview with George Barris

If you're in the mood for a little adventure, you're on the right track. As with most forms of entertainment, being an impersonator means an opportunity to travel. If you're on the West Coast, like I am, most of your overseas gigs will be to Asia. If you're on the East Coast, you're likely to get the chance to go to Europe. Not that it can't be the other way around, but bookers from Asia are more likely to call Los Angeles and Las Vegas for talent, whereas European bookers may have more contacts in New York. Having agents on both coasts, of course, increases

your traveling opportunities. As an impersonator, you are not limited to just one entertainment agent. In fact, you should have as many as possible. (Actors may have only one agent to book them in film or television, but for live entertainment, there is no limit.) You may at some point want to hire a manager or booking agent who will then deal with all of the other agencies or production companies that want your services, but you should probably be making triple figures before doing that.

A flyer from a Japanese show I did in 1998.

I have always loved to travel, so being an impersonator is a great job for me, and even in college I had a fascination with the Far East and had taken Asian studies courses. I never dreamed at that time that one day I would travel to China, Hong Kong, Taiwan, Thailand, Singapore, Malaysia, the Philippines, Korea, and Japan as a Marilyn Monroe impersonator! These journeys have given me some of the most interesting and meaningful experiences as an entertainer and as an individual. However, I don't want to mislead anyone. It's not always smooth sailing going to foreign lands, and it's not for everyone. It requires a lot of patience, flexibility, respect, and fascination for other cultures. Nothing makes me more furious than working with other artists overseas who still think they are in the United States and insult and criticize the local customs. When overseas, it's important to always be gracious and remember your role as a guest. To get to that point, entertainers must make sure their needs overseas have been negotiated and agreed to beforehand. Hotel or living arrangements, food requirements or per diem, travel and performance arrangements, and financial compensation (salaries for impersonators, domestic and internationally, range basically from $800 per week to $3,000 per week depending on your qualifications, the length of your show, and the budget of the client) must be spelled out in the contract so that there are no surprises and therefore nothing to dispute when finally in the foreign country. You should always receive a 50 percent deposit before going overseas. And your contract should be with a local agent who guarantees your salary regardless of whether or not it is paid by the overseas clients.

Enjoying the view from a cruise ship in Hong Kong Harbor when I was performing there in 1996.

For the most part, I have not had any major problems in my overseas jobs. The few problems I have had could have been prevented by better communication and negotiation prior to signing the contracts. A word of advice here from someone who has learned by making this mistake—never, never sign any contract for any job without reading it carefully and fully understanding and agreeing to everything in it. If there is something you don't feel comfortable with, then don't sign it. Perhaps have your own addendum already written up. (You may want to have an attorney review contracts for gigs involving a lot of money or overseas travel. But using common sense, working with licensed and bonded agencies, and getting that 50 percent deposit are your best insurance.)

Business aside, I have been treated extremely well overseas as an impersonator and just as myself. Marilyn, unfortunately, did not have the luxury of exploring Japan, Korea, or England without practically being mobbed, although she found a little more peace in Canada and Mexico. Impersonators have the benefit of getting star treatment (well, not quite the same as a real star) while in costume and then enjoying privacy while not in costume.

A Cherished Experience...

I traveled to Ponce, Puerto Rico, in July of 1998 to put on a show at a televised awards ceremony for local officials and executives. Well, the people of Puerto Rico don't let you come to their island without showing you a great time and making you feel like one of their family. Not only that—for the night's production, a multitude of stage crew, assistants, and show coordinators rushed to help with every part of my act, which included two costume changes, videotape of the real Marilyn projected above me, and a fan to blow under my white *Seven Year Itch* dress at just the right time. The night was a raging success, with cameramen and press swearing that I was Marilyn reincarnated (must have been the Puerto Rican rum). But what I treasure the most is that I had asked several crew members to videotape my performance with my video camera. When I returned to the U. S. and watched the tape, I found they had each videotaped their farewells and thanks to me. It is something I will always cherish.

Marketing Yourself

The title sounds clichéd, but getting actual work as a Monroe impersonator requires creating a professional package—consisting of pictures, résumé, bio, videotape, press clippings, and letters of reference—and mailing it out to as many entertainment agents, party planners, meeting planners, event consultants, and convention service companies as you can.

The most important of these are pictures and videotape. You can live without the rest, but without photos and video, you won't even get out of the starting gate. It takes time, so don't be discouraged.

My first Marilyn photos were shot in my apartment living room by a friend, and my first videotape was shot with a home video camera. But they got the ball rolling. These photos worked for a while, but I later had new ones taken by a professional photographer. As I gained experience and better costumes, I had still more photo shoots done. It is difficult to be satisfied with something that is always being compared with someone else and therefore can never be perfect. Your photos don't have to be clones of Marilyn. But they should capture the essence and energy of Marilyn and convey that you are a professional entertainer.

In order to accomplish this, I recommend you hire a makeup artist and hair/wig stylist if you are not comfortable doing it yourself, and have several pictures of Marilyn that you want to emulate. Study your own face in different light and at different angles to see what looks most like Marilyn—get other opinions also. Then meet with several professional photographers and look at their photos to see if their style is what you are after. A good price for two rolls of black-and-white film, including two eight-by-tens, would be $150 to $250 (these are Los Angeles prices and do not include hair and makeup, which could be $75 to $150 more).

In order to get good videotape of yourself performing live, you will probably have to volunteer to do some free performances and get a friend or relative with a video camera to tape it. Or you could go into a studio and have yourself professionally videotaped (I did that and it helped me to get my foot in the door). As you do more jobs, you will collect more videotape (often from producers or even audience members who videotape the show) and be able to put together a professional demo reel.

As for a résumé and bio (you may start out with only one or the other), you may have to enhance your experience and background a bit. I highly recommend using a professional writer for this. Then you must collect and make copies of press clippings and show programs for every Marilyn job you do. You can create your own publicity by being ambitious and creative and letting the local newspapers and television stations know where and when you're performing.

Your first package may only consist of a snapshot, a home video, and a letter. But eventually you should build up to a nice folder with your eight-by-ten photo glued neatly to the cover, and a résumé, bio, more pictures, cover letter, and copies of press clippings and show programs on the inside.

Now just who do you send all of these wonderful materials to after you've compiled them? You can start by looking in your local phone book under party planners, entertainment agencies, convention planners, destination resource management companies, and acting and talent agencies. Call them, tell them who you are and what you do, and ask if you can submit your package. If they handle impersonators or look-alikes, they won't say no. As I said before, you are not limited to just one agency. In fact, you need to be

with as many agencies as possible in order to get enough work. The reason is that many entertainment agencies handle all kinds of entertainment acts and may only occasionally have a request for a Marilyn.

There is no union governing impersonators, so there are no rules as to compensation, length of work day, or how much commission an agent may take (except in amusement parks, which have their own rules). You have to negotiate each job for yourself. Find out what the agency pays impersonators (and how much commission it takes). Try to meet the impersonators and ask them yourself so you get a good idea of the going rates in your area. Of course, never pay an agency any fee (unless they've booked you a job and you're paying them a commission), and always get a written contract for every job. You should also contact your local chamber of commerce, convention centers, and tourism boards directly to see if they will keep your package on file. These are just a few of the possibilities. Use your creativity and motivation to lead you in your own unique direction.

Posing with Jeane Carmen, a B movie goddess and sexy pinup girl who was a close friend of Marilyn in the years before she died. It was said that when the two were together, they looked like sisters.

CHAPTER FIVE

Those Who Have Dared

"Marilyn was like a sister I never had. The acting was like exhaling, like I released something."

Catherine Hicks

No one can deny the impact that Marilyn Monroe, her myth, and her image have had on art and popular culture. She has been the inspiration for countless biographies, paintings, cartoons, fiction novels, songs, television movies, and feature films. No doubt these all spring from our continued desire to understand her more fully and to gaze at her mesmerizing image of which we never seem to tire. What's more, this art has lured and continues to lure even the finest actresses into portraying Marilyn.

Madonna borrows from the Marilyn look.

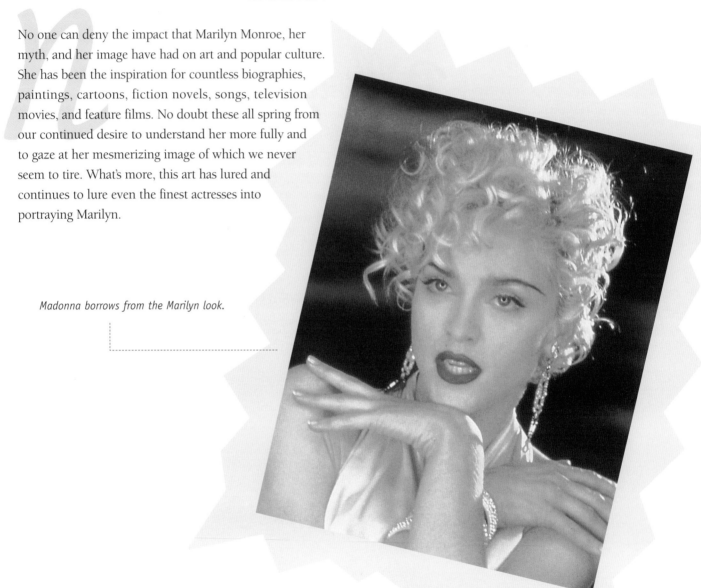

The HBO movie *Norma Jeane and Marilyn* saw Ashley Judd and Mira Sorvino taking on the task of becoming Marilyn. (The movie attempted to explain Marilyn in terms of her dual nature. She was a Gemini, and Geminis are supposedly many personalities rolled into one.) In the film, Ashley Judd plays a conniving, scheming Norma Jeane who is the critical voice inside Marilyn's head. Marilyn, played by Mira Sorvino, is the weak, vulnerable one, the alter ego created by Norma Jeane in order to gain the love and fame she desired. When interviewed in *People* magazine, Mira Sorvino had this to say about her relationship to the Marilyn Monroe she played:

> "...I loved that Marilyn was a little plump and didn't have to be an anorexic waif in order to be beautiful. She has some kind of immediate identification quality. You look at her, and you go with her. She's not foreign: she's simpatico....
>
> "She was an inspiration to me. A beacon. Her likability and accessibility validated my own wishes to be that way....In playing Marilyn I've gotten in touch with that side of me that loves being a woman and the particular power of that...."

Mira Sorvino

Judd and Sorvino both had to do an immense amount of research for their roles, especially Sorvino, who had the dream-come-true opportunity to imitate some of Marilyn's most famous scenes such as singing "Diamonds Are a Girl's Best Friend" and re-creating the white-dress scene from *The Seven Year Itch*. Playing Marilyn at such a high level no doubt comes with a lot of pressure, and while no one can ever be as good as the original, both actresses earned Golden Globe nominations for their roles in the movie. In the same *People* interview, Judd made these conclusions about Marilyn Monroe and what her research had revealed:

"I've come to regard the standard things that are said about [Marilyn] as profundities instead of blithe statements. Her search for a daddy, the sexual vulnerability in each of her performances—these things are sincerely true. I don't radically veer from the canonized mythology of Marilyn Monroe. But I have become more tenderhearted and sympathetic to it...."

Ashley Judd

Of course, not every portrayal of Marilyn has her coming out squeaky clean. TV soap star Melody Anderson starred as Marilyn in the 1993 USA World Premiere Movie *Marilyn & Bobby: Her Final Affair,* which presented a "fictionalized account inspired by the public lives of Marilyn Monroe and Robert F. Kennedy" (the disclaimer at the beginning of the film). Some critics were offended at the notion that the two may have had an affair or that there could have been surveillance and involvement by the Teamsters, the Mafia, FBI Director J. Edgar Hoover, etc., and came down hard on the picture for what they called "docudrama shamelessness" and "another crude cash-in on Marilyn Monroe and the Kennedys." Marilyn's relationships with the Kennedys is a subject that won't be undertaken in this book. So it's up to the viewers to decide for themselves on this one.

Melody Anderson

In September 1991, ABC aired its Sunday night movie, *Marilyn & Me*, a film based on Robert Slatzer's account of his lifelong relationship with Marilyn and their brief and secret marriage in Mexico prior to her superstardom. Impersonator Susan Griffiths played Marilyn, Jesse Dabson was Slatzer, and Joel Grey (Best Supporting Actor, *Cabaret*, 1972) played agent Johnny Hyde. The movie and the actors' performances received rave reviews, and Susan Griffiths bore a striking resemblance to Marilyn. However, some discredit Slatzer's claim of the marriage, citing lack of evidence.

Susan Griffiths, who has been impersonating Marilyn since she was a teenager, said that her resemblance to Marilyn was first discovered at a Halloween party in high school where she had donned a blonde wig. (It could happen to you!) She also said that she had to eat a lot (ah, the perks!) to "keep Marilyn's fullness in her face."

Marilyn Monroe impersonator Susan Griffiths.

Not every movie about Marilyn Monroe is a dramatization of her life. Other films explore her impact on people and culture. *Calendar Girl* was a movie that was indirectly about Marilyn and featured a Monroe impersonator. It starred Jason Priestly, Jerry O'Connell, and Gabriel Olds as three friends who embark on a journey to Hollywood in the summer of 1962 in hopes of meeting Marilyn. They run into a series of misadventures along the way, including a trip to a nude beach and a run-in with the Mafia. They eventually get their unforgettable encounter with Marilyn, who was played by impersonator Stephanie Anderson (vocals were done by Courtney Page), whose face remains mostly shrouded in the film. (Stephanie Anderson had also played Marilyn in an edition of "Hard Copy.") In *Calendar Girl,* the sweet, approachable, sexy, girl-next-door image of Monroe is kept intact, and the effect she had directly and indirectly on the three coming-of-age boys mirrors the strong effect she had and still has today.

Marilyn impersonator Stephanie Anderson.

The 1985 art film *Insignificance*, which starred Theresa Russell, proposed a fictitious what-if plot where the paths of Marilyn (Russell), Albert Einstein (Michael Emil), Senator Joe McCarthy (Tony Curtis), Joe DiMaggio (Gary Busey), and a character called the Indian (Will Sampson) meet in bizarre circumstances, one of which has Marilyn propositioning Einstein and explaining to him the theory of relativity. To prepare for the role, Theresa Russell took voice lessons to raise the tone of her naturally low, husky voice. "I watched all her films and read everything I could get my hands on," Russell told me.

The 1980 ABC movie special *Marilyn: The Untold Story* starred Catherine Hicks, then a New York actress who had played Dr. Faith Coleridge for two years in the ABC soap *"Ryan's Hope."* Hicks already had played leading roles in the theater in *Bus Stop* (playing Cherie—the same part Marilyn made famous) and *After the Fall*, Arthur Miller's

play based on his four-year marriage to Marilyn. To prepare for the film role, Hicks had to gain weight, which she did by eating more than her share of doughnuts for breakfast. Her hair had to be bleached and her breasts amply padded.

Actress Catherine Hicks played Marilyn in the 1980 ABC movie special Marilyn: The Untold Story.

Hicks said of the experience, "I don't know if I'd like to be voluptuous all the time, but I did feel a certain extra femininity that was fun, and it was a joy to have my dress billowing in the breeze." In addition to remaking the *Seven Year Itch* subway scene, Hicks also replicated the *Something's Got to Give* swimming pool scene by swimming in the nude. However, that scene was made exclusively for overseas consumption!

In the film *Finding Graceland* (1998) actress Bridget Fonda took on the task of playing a Marilyn Monroe *impersonator*. Fortunately for me, there was no book out then on how to impersonate Marilyn, which gave me the opportunity to discuss the subject with Bridget. Of course, she not only had to study Marilyn herself (and everything that we go through in the rest of this book), but she also had to study a Marilyn impersonator! She was particularly interested in knowing about life on the road, whether I felt like Marilyn twenty-four hours a day, seven days a week, and if I ever "fell for" Elvis impersonators. In the end, I think I learned more from Bridget than she did from me as I watched her dissect Marilyn's dance moves and mannerisms and reconstruct her routine of "You'd Be Surprised" in a singing voice that I couldn't distinguish from Marilyn herself!

Bridget Fonda played a Marilyn Monroe impersonator in Finding Graceland.

Many other actresses have taken on the task of portraying Marilyn or characters based on her, such as Connie Stevens in the 1974 film *The Sex Symbol* and Faye Dunaway in the play *After the Fall*; Linda Kerridge in *Fade to Black*, 1980 (Kerridge played a Monroe look-alike); Stephanie Lawrence in *Marilyn!* (1983); Alyson Reed in *Marilyn: An American Fable* (1983); Misty Rowe in *Goodbye Norma Jean* (1976); and Paula Lane in *Goodnight Sweet Marilyn* (1989).

Lenore Zahn stepped to the plate in the 1979 stage play *Hey, Marilyn*, and Katie LaBourdette wrote and starred in the play *Sleepless Nights*.

For talk show appearances, Cindy Crawford has dressed up like Marilyn for Halloween, while Madonna has done music videos ("Material Girl") and photo spreads imitating Marilyn's look in minute detail (see "Homage to Norma Jean," *Vanity Fair,* April, 1991.)

Marilyn impersonator
Barbara Bogar.

"I was a singer in 'Jubilee' at Bally's, Las Vegas, when a routine stop at the hairdresser's changed my life. A performer from Legends in Concert™ was sitting next to me and remarked that my voice sounded like Marilyn Monroe's and suggested that I audition with Legends. I had never done an impression of Marilyn, or anyone else for that matter, and had no Marilyn lines or songs to do but decided to try it just for fun. At the audition, I sang a couple of standards with the band and was taken by surprise when I was hired."

Barbara Bogar,
Las Vegas

The Academy Award–winning movie *The Apartment* features a Marilyn look-alike. Ray Walston says to Jack Lemmon regarding her, "Listen, kid, I can't pass this up. She looks like Marilyn Monroe!" Scores of other films, television shows, music videos, and commercials have had bit parts played by Monroe impersonators or look-alikes, including *Pulp Fiction* (Susan Griffiths as Monroe), HBO's *The Rat Pack*, and *Introducing Dorothy Dandridge*. And I have been fortunate enough to nab a few parts for myself. I've appeared in Roger Corman's *Munchie Strikes Back*; Showtime's *Out There*, TV's "Clueless," The Rembrandts music video "This House Is Not a Home"; and a Capri Sun™ fruit drink commercial.

What's more, the "Marilyn" roles don't show signs of dying out any time soon. America is hooked on nostalgia, and the whole world is hooked on Marilyn Monroe. What Vegas revue show isn't enhanced by using a Monroe look-alike? Who wouldn't give their undivided attention to any commercial, video, or TV show using Marilyn's image? And with so many films constantly being made about the fifties and sixties, there are bound to be more "Marilyn" roles. Who knows? If you find yourself all dressed up in the right place at the right time—your golden locks styled with that bouncy, flirtatious curl, and your luscious, red lips shimmering under the lights—then give a wink, pucker up, blow a big kiss, and wave! One of those roles could belong to you!

Marilyn impersonator Elaine Chez models the original dress from Some Like It Hot *for Christie's in New York.*

Merchandise created using Marilyn's image includes calendars, puzzles, posters, wine, datebooks, mugs, collectors' dolls, ink stamps, Christmas ornaments, watches, lingerie, clocks, collector plates, wrapping paper, refrigerator magnets, T-shirts, gift bags, puzzles, jewelry, Barbie dolls, perfume, eyewear, greeting cards, stationery, socks, neckties, linens, phone cards, desk covers, diaries, and much more.

A young, fresh-faced Marilyn Monroe.

Marilyn was an excellent impersonator herself, as photographs of her by renowned photographer Richard Avedon reveal. Taken in 1958, they show Marilyn portraying Lillian Russell, Theda Bara, Clara Bow, and Jean Harlow. Marilyn captured each star's essence, look, and attitude with amazing precision. She said she was more proud of those photos than of anything else she had ever done.

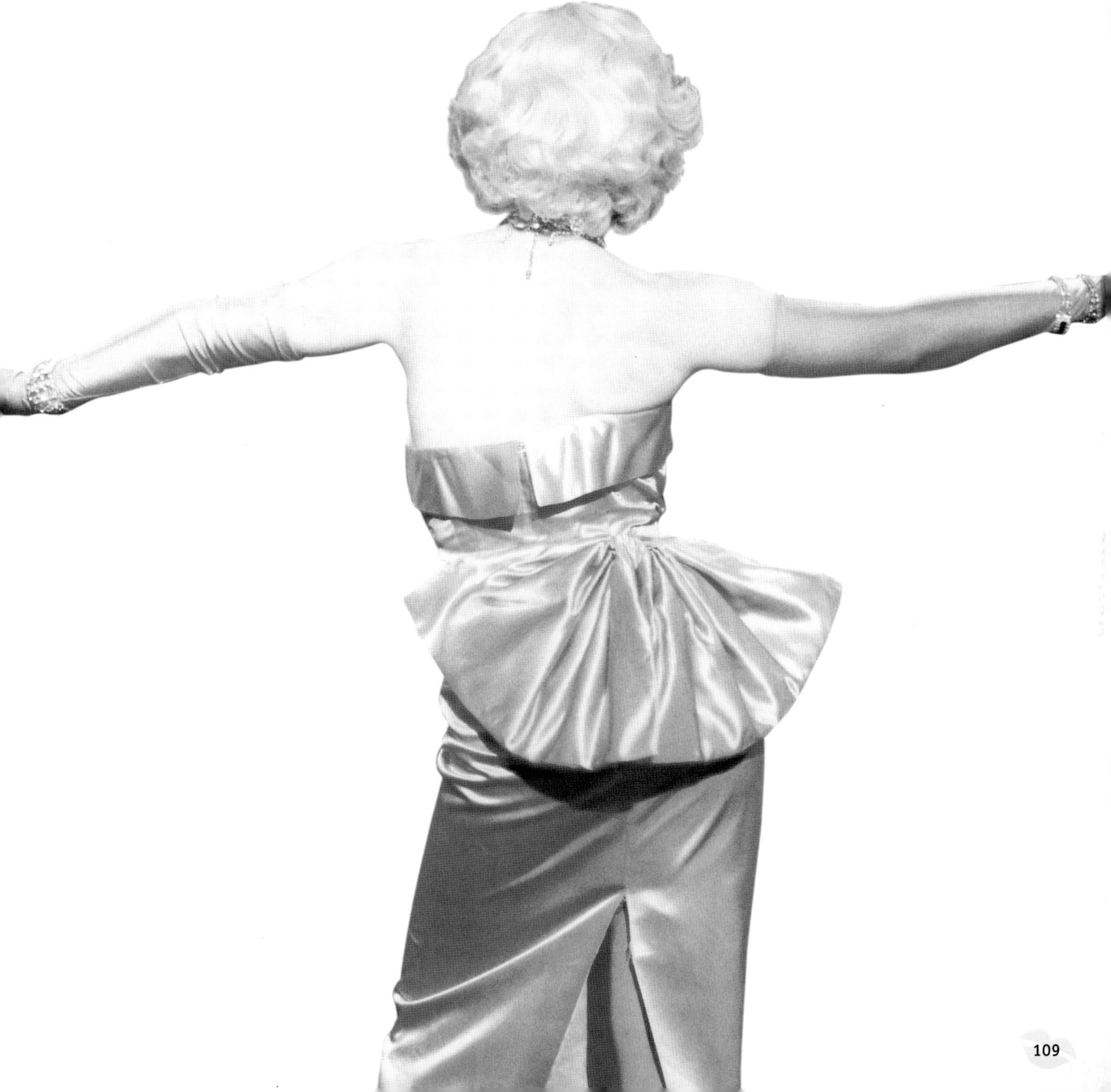

RESOURCES

Where to Find It...

Dress patterns

White *Seven Year Itch*: called "Blonde Bombshell"—not identical to the original, but close—available mail-order through AlterYears for the Costumer. (626) 585-2994. $16.95. Also try Simplicity's white *Seven Year Itch* and pink strapless pattern, #8393. (888) 588-2700. (Price varies.)

Strapless, backless bustier

Various brands in white or nude at J. C. Penney's, Sears, Macy's. . .from $16.99 to $34.99.

Backup tape of Marilyn songs by Pocket Songs

In most karaoke stores. . .$12.98.

Marilyn videos

Gentlemen Prefer Blondes, *Some Like It Hot*, *The Seven Year Itch*, *There's No Business Like Show Business*, *How to Marry a Millionaire*, *The River of No Return*—available for rent at video stores. For sale at $19.99 each.

For information on how to obtain rare footage, video clips, and film of Marilyn, including her performances to troops in Korea, write to R. R. Rees, 20806 Park Canyon, Katy, Texas 77450.

Marilyn Fan Clubs

The following is a list of just a few of the Marilyn fan clubs in the world:

The Legend Club for Marilyn Monroe
c/o Dale Notinelli
2401 Artesia Blvd., #185
Redondo Beach, CA 90278

Marilyn Remembered
c/o Greg Schreiner
1237 Carmona Street
Los Angeles, CA 90019
(213) 931-3337

Marilyn Reporter
c/o Debbie Jasgur
1648 S. Crystal Lake Drive, Suite 40
Orlando, FL 32806
(407) 898-6387

Marilyn Monroe Fan Club
c/o Michelle Finn
14 Clifton Sq.
Corby, Northants, NN17 2DB   Great Britain

Marilyn Monroe Fan Club (Australia)
P.O. Box 60
Richmond, VIC Australia 3121

Agencies

Here are a couple of very reputable look-alike/impersonator agencies in Los Angeles:

Mulligan Management
11169 Morrison Street
North Hollywood, CA 91601
(818) 752-9474

Celebrity Look-Alikes by Elyse
69-930 Highway 111, Suite 300
Rancho Mirage, CA 92270
(888) 771-6611

Elaine Chez Company
P.O. Box 2242
Astoria, New York 11102
(718) 956-7287

Entertainment Contractors
P.O. Box 65151
Los Angeles, CA 90065
(323) 256-9613

There are dozens more, so get the Yellow Pages for Los Angeles or whatever city you want to work in!

For full production shows contact:

Ron Stein's Hollywood Stars
P.O. Box 956
Alta Loma, CA 91701
(909) 941-1797

Reading About Marilyn

Barris, George. *Marilyn, Her Life in Her Own Words*. New York: Henry Holt & Co., 1995.

Bernard, Susan, editor. *Bernard of Hollywood's Marilyn*. New York: St. Martin's Press, 1993.

Carroll, Jack. *Falling for Marilyn: The Lost Niagara Collection*. New York: Michael Friedman Publishing Group, 1996.

Chierichetti, David. *Hollywood Costume Design*. New York: Harmony Books, 1976.

Clark, Colin. *The Prince, the Showgirl, and Me*. New York: St. Martin's Press, 1996.

Conway, Ricci. *The Complete Films of Marilyn Monroe*. New York: Carol Publishing Group, 1994.

Cunningham, Ernest W. *The Ultimate Marilyn*. Los Angeles: Renaisance Books, 1998.

Dougherty, James E. *The Secret Happiness of Marilyn Monroe*. Chicago: Playboy, 1976.

Fox, Patty. *Star Style: Hollywood Legends as Fashion Icons*. Los Angeles: Angel City, 1995.

Fuller, Graham. Interviews with Ashley Judd and Mira Sorvino. *Interview*, February 1996.

Greene, Milton. *Milton's Marilyn*. Munich: Schirmer, 1994.

Guilaroff, Sidney. *Crowning Glory*. Los Angeles: General, 1996.

Guiles, Fred Lawrence. *Legend: The Life and Death of Marilyn Monroe*. New York: Stein, 1984.

Harrison, Jay. *Marilyn*. New Jersey: CLB International, 1997.

Haspiel, James. *The Young Marilyn: Becoming the Legend*. New York: Hyperion, 1994.

Jackovich, Karen G. "After Going to Bed as Marilyn Monroe, Unheralded Catherine Hicks May Wake Up a Star." *People Magazine*, September 1980.

Jasgur, Sakol. *The Birth of Marilyn*. Great Britain: Sidgwich & Jackson Limited, 1991.

Leahy, Michael. "Meet the New Marilyn." *TV Guide*, September 1991.

"Marilyn: Something's Got to Give" (television special). Fox Entertainment News, Inc., 1990.

Pepitone, Lena, with William Stadiem. *Marilyn Monroe Confidential*. New York: Simon & Schuster, 1979.

Riese, Randall, and Neal Hitchens. *The Unabridged Marilyn: Her Life from A to Z*. New York: Congdon, 1987.

Rooks-Denes, Kathy. *Marilyn*. New York: Bantam Doubleday Dell, 1993.

Rosten, Norman. *Marilyn: An Untold Story*. New York: Signet, 1973.

Spoto, Donald. "Marilyn & Bobby" (review). *TV Guide*, July 1993.

Stern, Bert. *The Last Sitting, a Selection*. New York: William Morrow & Co., 1982.

Strasberg, Susan. *Marilyn and Me: Sisters, Rivals, Friends*. New York: Warner Books, 1992.

Summers, Anthony. *Goddess: The Secret Lives of Marilyn Monroe*. New York: Macmillan, 1985.

Ventura, Michael. *Marilyn Monroe from Beginning to End*. London: Blandford Press, 1997.

Wetherby, W. J. *Conversations with Marilyn*. New York: Mason, 1976.

Wilder, Billy, and I. A. L. Diamond. *Some Like It Hot, the Screenplay*. New York: Signet, 1959.

About the Author

Gailyn Addis began her entertainment career when she was a student studying Chinese and modeling in Taipei, Taiwan. In 1994, she moved to Los Angeles to study acting, dance, and voice. Her physical resemblance to Marilyn Monroe was soon discovered, as well as her ability to impersonate the voices and looks of Marilyn, Judy Garland, Madonna, Liza Minnelli, Olivia Newton-John, Alanis Morissette, and many others.

She has since stacked up an impressive list of credits in film, TV, and music video, portraying Marilyn in Showtime's *Out There*, the Disney Channel's *Munchie Strikes Back*, the TV shows "Clueless," "The Other Side," and "The Mommies," and the music videos of the Rembrandts and Ministry. She got the cover of the March 1994 issue of *Private Club Magazine*, and has been the subject of newspaper articles and TV interviews both locally and internationally.

Overseas venues where Gailyn has performed include the Olympic Stadium in Seoul, Korea, the Genting Highlands Resort in Malaysia, the Bangkok Royal Sports Club, the Prince Hotels in Japan, American military bases all over the world, and the Star Cruises in Hong Kong with the highly acclaimed Legends in Concert™.

In the United States, she lights up the stage in *The Really Big Show* at the Tropicana in Atlantic City and Ron Stein's *Hollywood Stars* at Caesars' Palace, Lake Tahoe, Bally's, and the Chinook Winds casinos. She has also made special appearances for Legends in Concert, Mercedes Benz, McDonalds, Universal Studios, Paramount Pictures, and the Debbie Reynolds Hotel & Casino for which she modeled the original *Seven Year Itch* dress worn by Marilyn Monroe (it was a perfect fit!).

As if that isn't enough, Gailyn also writes and produces her own original music. With her sultry, risk-taking style, she has produced a CD in the alternative pop-rock genre that is generating a stir on the Los Angeles music scene. Gailyn Addis is represented by Brian Mulligan of Mulligan Management, 11167 Morrison St., North Hollywood, CA 91601, (818) 752-9474. Visit Gailyn's music Web site at www.gailynaddis.com.

Photo Credits

Shooting Star, Hollywood, California
Pages V, VI, 2, 6, 9, 19, 20, 29, 31, 44, 55, 58, 98. 99, 101, 104, 108.

Zuma Press, Inc.
Page 100.

Courtesy of Rick Marino
Page 105.

Ryan Beck
Pages 41 and 50.

Hiroyoshi Kawano
Page 77.

Courtesy of Brandon James and Jeanne Carmen
Page 95.

Evon Shahan, New View Photography
Page 102.

Courtesy of Jay Ramsey
Page 106.

Jim Carrol
Page 107.

Courtesy of Ron Stein
Page 114.

Courtesy of the Museum of Natural History, San Diego, California
Pages 61 and 86.

All other photography of Gailyn Addis as Marilyn Monroe by Jeff Hyman.

Acknowledgments

My thanks to Rick Marino for presenting me with this opportunity; to Marilyn for being so worthy of imitation; to photographer Jeff Hyman for really "delivering"; to Marilyn lookalikes Susan Griffiths, Stephanie Anderson, Barbara Bogar, Dena Drotar, Holly Beavon, Diana Dawn, and Elaine Chez for sharing their stories and photos; to Theresa Russell, Catherine Hicks, and Bridget Fonda; to photographer Hiroyoshi Kawano; to Ron Stein and his Hollywood Stars show; to the San Diego Museum of Natural History; to all of my agents, my husband Mike, my family, everyone at becker&mayer!, Sourcebooks Publishing, and to Marilyn Monroe fans all over the world.